INALIENABLE RIGHTS: A DEFENSE

Inalienable Rights: A Defense

Diana T. Meyers

Columbia University Press
New York   1985

The Hull Memorial Publication Fund of Cornell University has aided the publication of this book.

Columbia University Press
New York   Guildford, Surrey
Copyright © 1985 Columbia University Press
All rights reserved

Printed in the United States of America

Library of Congress Cataloging in Publication Data

Meyers, Diana T.
  Inalienable rights.

  Bibliography: p.
  Includes index.
  1. Civil rights.   2. Natural law.   I. Title.
JC571.M454   1985   323.4   84-23007
ISBN 0-231-06034-3
ISBN 0-231-06035-1 (pbk.)
Clothbound editions of Columbia University Press books are Smyth-sewn and printed on permanent and durable acid-free paper.

To Lewis

Contents

Acknowledgments	ix
Chapter 1: The Problem of Natural Rights	1
1. Traditional Characterizations of Human Rights	2
2. The Moral Import of Rights Possession	4
3. Forms of Rights Loss	9
4. Sources of Criteria for Inalienable Rights	15
Chapter 2: A Contribution of Inalienable Rights to the Adequacy of Moral Systems	23
1. Varieties of Rights Renunciation	23
2. Conscientious Renunciation	28
3. Obligation, Supererogation, and Rights	34
4. The Inadequacy of Self-defeating Moral Systems	37
5. Inadmissible Obligations	44
6. Admissible Permissions	48
7. Inalienable Rights	51
Chapter 3: Four Inalienable Rights	53
1. The Right to Life and the Right to Personal Liberty	54
2. Force, Liberties, and Law	56
3. The Right to Benign Treatment and the Right to Satisfaction of Basic Needs	62
4. Supererogatory Pain and Deprivation	65

5. A Note on Property Rights	68
6. Supererogation and Promising	71
7. Personal Worth and Personal Codes	76

Chapter 4: Inalienable Rights and the Foundations of Moral Interaction — 83

1. Rescission by Design	84
2. Inalienable Liberties	87
3. Justifying Self-interested Deceit	93
4. Impenetrable Deceit	98
5. Amoral Action and Enforced Irresponsibility	102
6. Two Types of Rescission by Design	111

Chapter 5: Possession of Inalienable Rights — 115

1. Species Membership and the Qualifications for Inalienable Rights	116
2. The Equality of Inalienable Rights	122
3. The Dispossessed	127
4. Children	128
5. Animals	136
6. The Universality of Inalienable Rights	140

Chapter 6: Permissible Abridgment — 143

1. Varieties of Abridgment	143
2. The Wrong of Denial	149
3. The Problem of Enforcement	152
4. The Injustice of Private Enforcement	157
5. Enforcement and the State	163
6. The Imposition of Punishment	165
7. State Implementation of Subsistence Rights	169
8. The Difference Between Inalienable Rights and Obligations of Noninterference and Aid	175
9. The Ineliminability of Inalienable Rights	180

Chapter 7: Contract Theory and Inalienable Rights — 183

1. Defending Natural Rights	183
2. Political Ideals	188
3. Individualism	192

Notes	197
Bibliography	209
Index	213

Acknowledgments

I have benefited greatly from others' help on this essay. At different stages, Gertrude Ezorsky, Virginia Held, Peter Katzenstein, David Lyons, Lewis Meyers, and Richard Wasserstrom read and commented on the entire manuscript. Also, I presented parts of the manuscript to colloquia at Cornell University, S.U.N.Y. at Stony Brook, the University of Colorado at Boulder, and the University of Kansas at Lawrence, and I received valuable suggestions on each occasion. David Armstrong's and Michael Busch's help preparing the typescript has been indispensable.

My article "The Rationale for Inalienable Rights in Moral Systems," *Social Theory and Practice* (Summer 1981), 7(2):127–143 is reprinted with permission.

A note on style: We have yet to find a felicitous and nonsexist third person singular pronoun. As a compromise between feminist principle and graceful style, I have adopted the rule of using the masculine pronoun generically in most of the text but using the feminine pronoun in all examples, in mentions of special cases, and in extended explorations of hypothetical cases.

Inalienable Rights: A Defense

1

The Problem of Natural Rights

The idea of a natural right has exerted a powerful influence over the course of political history and the development of political philosophy. Yet, persistent doubts about the intelligibility of this concept have dogged natural rights whenever they have been invoked. Their association with theologically based natural law doctrines and with the state of nature component of contract theory has made persons unsympathetic to these metaethical positions suspicious. Nevertheless, the fundamental normative load carried by natural rights—that persons ought to be guaranteed a core of personal security and autonomy—is almost irresistible. Freeing natural rights from extraneous and unwanted metaethical reverberations while preserving and embellishing their attractive moral content, many philosophers have adopted the label 'human rights' and have argued that various metaethical positions can accommodate them. These advances notwithstanding, the idea of a human right has resisted analysis, and lists of human rights have defied systematic defense. It is the aim of this essay to allay doubts about the existence of human rights by establishing an analysis of inalienable rights on the basis of which a set of inalienable rights can be defended.

1. Traditional Characterizations of Human Rights

Tradition supplies three ways of characterizing human rights. Almost invariably, they are said to be universal, that is, all persons have them. Sometimes it has been claimed that they are absolute; in other words, no one can ever justifiably abridge them. Alternatively, they have been portrayed as inalienable, which is to say it is impossible for anyone who has these rights to lose them.[1]

That universality within the domain of humans and only within this domain is a necessary condition for human rights seems to be built into the very terminology that denotes them. Still, invoking this property to account for these rights is not helpful since universality is as problematic a concept from a normative point of view as human rights themselves are. The trouble lies initially in justifying the domain of universality. Should the domain include all human beings regardless of their differences? If all human beings belong to it, then why not all sentient creatures? Which domain seems appropriate depends to a large extent on which rights—compare, for example, the right to an education with the right to benign treatment—are being proffered. Unfortunately, the domain of individuals who have human rights poses a moral question which cannot be settled by fiat. Thus, focusing on universality shifts the problem from discerning which rights are human rights to the problem of finding a defensible basis for circumscribing the domain in which human rights are universally possessed. Furthermore, since handling this preliminary problem would not take care of the remaining problems of ascertaining which rights all members of the domain of universality have and explaining why they have these rights, it is clear that the idea of universality cannot alone found a theory of human rights.

Some advocates of human rights have relied on the notion of an absolute right to supplement the idea of universality. This theory maintains that human rights are those that all members of the domain of universality have because no one can ever legitimately refuse to acknowledge these rights and honor claims based upon them. On this view, human rights are functions of inflexible obligations, for the class of human rights is distinguished by the class of correlative obligations which are immune to countervailing considerations.

This suggestion quickly falls prey to counterexamples featuring situations in which two allegedly absolute rights conflict so that one must give way to the other. Objections of this sort spurred Bentham's snide, if amusing, dismissal of human rights as "nonsense upon stilts." Nevertheless, there have been various attempts to rehabilitate this account by admitting only one vaguely formulated human right, by including the circumstances under which a plurality of human rights may be justifiably infringed in the formulations of the rights, or by analyzing human rights as prima facie rights which impose a duty on others only to give consideration to them in the course of deliberation. Though these modifications take the sting out of Bentham's critique, they also weaken the notion of absoluteness so much that few rights would not count as absolute rights. Evidently, absoluteness is either too feeble or too strong to serve as a criterion for human rights.

Absoluteness fails as an account of human rights because there is no intermediate level of obligatory respect for rights between inviolability and susceptibility to justifiable abridgment. To be sure, there are degrees of susceptibility or, put the other way around, degrees of stringency. But a single right's stringency rating may vary for different people or under different circumstances.[2] For example, the stringency of a murderous assailant's right to life plummets toward zero, whereas the stringency of an innocent person's right to life usually approaches infinity. Enormous as these stringency fluctuations are for all rights, it is impossible to demarcate a category of almost absolute rights.

Eluding the unmanageable problems about respecting rights raised by the criterion of absoluteness, universality concentrates instead on possession of rights. A right may be universally possessed though it is not generally acknowledged as such and though it may be respected in unforeseeable ways.

Unfortunately, since a right's universality could be a mere coincidence, universality could prove trivial unless it is tied to an account of why all persons have certain rights. The concept of universality is not rich enough to supply the missing explanation, but the idea of an inalienable right, which has received surprisingly little attention despite the inadequacies of other approaches, is an obvious place to turn for it.

Like universality, inalienability adopts the perspective of the right-holder rather than the right-respecter: an inalienable right is one that the right-holder cannot lose regardless of what he does or how others treat him and even if others are justified in declining to grant him what he demands in exercising his right. But unlike an affirmation of universality, an affirmation of inalienability presupposes an explanation of what it is about inalienable rights and the individuals who possess these rights that holds them together. While separating the problem of explicating human rights from the thornier problem of what duties these rights impose on others, the concept of inalienability yields an account of the traditionally emphasized connection between the properties of right-holders and human rights.

2. The Moral Import of Rights Possession

The project of establishing a set of inalienable rights might seem insufficiently ambitious because inalienable rights that are not absolute do not provide right-holders with any immutable moral guarantees. As elemental constants of moral relations, human rights, it might be thought, must definitively rule out some ways of mistreating people and unconditionally require that people be accorded certain desirable types of treatment. Otherwise, what good are these rights to flesh and blood, vulnerable but ever aspiring human beings? Perhaps, the admission that there are no rights that are both substantive and absolute is a decisive ground for concluding that there are no human rights at all, not a reason to rely on the idea of an inalienable right.

If possession of rights had no moral import apart from the right-holder's enjoyment of the object of his right, the line of thought sketched above would be persuasive. But since the position of a person who has a right that has been superseded by conflicting considerations is not equivalent to that of a person who has no right, and since the position of a person who has an inalienable right differs from that of a person whose right may be renounced or otherwise voided, the reputed constancy of human rights can be located in the manner of their possession.[3]

It has often been remarked that a person's possession of a right entails only a prima facie obligation to deliver the object of the right to him on demand or not to interfere with his enjoyment of the object of the right. Moral considerations independent of an individual's right may outweigh the obligations correlative to his right and thus may take precedence. Yet, the distinction between an absolute right and an inalienable right would collapse if the justifiability of infringing a right entailed an obligation on the part of the right-holder to relinquish his right. Moreover, anyone nefariously seeking to deprive a right-holder of a right could achieve his aim simply by manipulating circumstances so as to permit infringement of the right. Unless rights survived the vicissitudes of circumstances, they would provide no protection for right-holders beyond what wit and fortune in conjunction with others' probity and indulgence already secure. Rights, then, would be superfluous. Though the justifiability of overriding a person's right may sharply reduce the right's stringency, it does not extinguish the right. Consequently, adverse circumstances never absolve potential right-respecters of all responsibility toward the right-holder.

Prior to any decision to withhold the object of a person's right, the right-holder is entitled to assert his right, and others cannot legitimately suppress or ignore his claims in deliberating about how to proceed. In informal settings, we feel morally bound to give right-holders a sympathetic audience. In official settings, this obligation is codified in procedures, such as the safeguards of a fair trial which assure the defendant, whose rights may be abridged if she is convicted and punished, that her rights-based claims will receive an impartial hearing. Furthermore, since rights constitute distinctively firm moral protections, they may be overridden only if especially powerful reasons support this course of action.[4] Accordingly, prospective right-respecters must contend with the force of the rights involved in the predicaments they face. In short, rights and the claims they sponsor are never negligible.

Still, it must be asked what remains of an abridged right, that is, what options remain to the right-holder and what obligations the right imposes on others, in the aftermath of abridgment. Roughly, abridged rights require acknowledgment of the right-holder—even a right-holder who, arguably, should have waived his right—as a victim, and they entitle the right-holder to claim this aggrieved status and its consolations. Depending on the seriousness of the injury to the right-holder, the circumstances in which the injury was inflicted, and the resources subsequently available to make amends, acknowledgment of the victim can assume various forms ranging from offering explanations or apologies to awarding compensation and protection from further injury. Whatever type of acknowledgment is appropriate, the right-holder may not be dismissed out of hand.

Of course, situations may arise in which the right-holder's victimization cannot be acknowledged because others have more pressing duties or because the right-holder can no longer be reached by his victimizers or their agents. However, this reminder that no duty is absolute shows not that rights evaporate under inauspicious circumstances but rather that not all wrongs can be assuaged, much less erased. To abridge a person's right is to wrong him though not necessarily to act wrongly. To fail, moreover, to acknowledge this injury is to deny his right though not to destroy it. When all modes of respect for a person's rights are closed, the situation is morally intractable. The difference between being a right-holder and being without

The Problem of Natural Rights   7

rights in such an impasse is two-fold: a right-holder is permitted to remonstrate with others about his misfortune and also to insist that others take steps to prevent such harms or to shoulder any similar burdens in the future. While kindness to others or prudent regard for his own interests may dictate forgoing these measures, his right entitles him to take them.

Rights do not ordain precisely what conduct is required to respect them in various circumstances. Nevertheless, their moral force is considerable. They establish a presumption against abridgment and in favor of right-holders' resistance to abridgment which affords individuals a counterweight to social goals.[5] Moreover, they establish a backup presumption against ignoring abridgments and in favor of right-holders' voicing their grievances. Together, these presumptions guard the interests of right-holders and validate their adamant concern with these interests. Inalienable rights seal this protection from loss.

A person whose right is inalienable does not enjoy more prerogatives than a person whose right is alienable. On the contrary, he enjoys one fewer since he cannot get rid of those he has. Persons holding alienable rights may be induced by conscience, inclination, or anticipated gains to give up their rights by renouncing, conditionally waiving, or transferring them. Also, alienable rights may be forfeitable, and persons other than the right-holder may have the authority to revoke these rights. Having disposed of a right or having had it taken from him, a person will, on balance, be satisfied with, indifferent to, or disappointed in his rightless state. Inalienable rights protect right-holders from ill-advised disavowals and damaging revocations at the price of depriving these individuals of any gratifications that might be obtained through alienation of their rights. Though the protections secured by these rights are not absolute, inalienable rights ensure that abridgments will not be neutralized by the cooperation of the right-holder or the connivance of others.

It is, however, important to notice that inalienable rights can be exercised in various ways. As we have seen, exercising a right can take the form of demanding the good conferred by the right and using or enjoying that good or, in unfavorable circumstances, demanding acknowledgment as a victim and taking the benefits of this status. But persons can also exercise rights by refraining from asserting them.

When a person pointedly refrains from asserting an alienable right, it can be surmised that the right-holder wishes to renounce, conditionally waive, or transfer the right. Precisely how a right-holder's self-restraint is to be understood depends on the surrounding circumstances and on customary practices governing the right. Nevertheless, prolonged and intentional silence that effectively permits abridgment of an alienable right eradicates the wrong of abridgment.[6] In contrast, the definition of inalienable rights rules out reading a right-holder's mute submission to abridgment as implicit renunciation, conditional waiver, or transfer. Thus, abridgment of an inalienable right necessarily wrongs the right-holder. Still, his willing toleration of this treatment may not be devoid of moral import, for under appropriate circumstances it may properly be interpreted as forgiving the wrong visited upon him. Although no right-holder has the power to transform the injury of an abridged inalienable right into a morally neutral event, right-holders can pardon abridgments and can decline acknowledgment as victims.

Whereas an alienable right permits right-holders to repudiate their moral attachment to the object of the right, an inalienable right bars right-holders from divesting themselves of their moral ties to the object of the right. Because a right-holder cannot cease to be entitled to the good an inalienable right confers on him, he cannot escape the option of exercising the right. The ubiquity of this option imposes on him a share of the responsibility for the course of his relations to the object of the right. Lacking the object of his right, he may seek to obtain it or decide not to pursue it; offered the object of his right, he may accept or refuse it;[7] deprived of the object of his right, he may claim victimization or forgive the abridgment. It would be foolish to suppose that this array of options endows persons with complete control over the object of any right and therefore with full responsibility for their enjoyment or nonenjoyment of this good. An entitlement to press claims is no guarantee of winning them. Nevertheless, this entitlement discredits cries of overpowering mistreatment in the wake of apathetic submission and sustains belated protests whenever right-holders' claims have been forcibly suppressed.

Possession of inalienable rights enters right-holders as participants in all situations in which these rights figure. Thus, the constant moral significance of inalienable rights stems neither from invariant respect for these rights nor from uniform exercise of them. Rather, it consists of the acknowledgment of a set of invariably legitimate interests shared by all right-holders along with a morally inextricable measure of autonomy in regard to these interests.

3. Forms of Rights Loss

Rights do not conveniently vanish when circumstances justify overriding them, but there are ways for persons to lose rights. The mechanisms of rights loss include renunciation whereby the right-holder simply disavows his right, conditional waiver whereby the right-holder temporarily suspends his right, transfer whereby the right-holder gives, trades, or sells his right to another individual, forfeiture whereby the right-holder ceases to qualify for possession of his right, and revocation whereby someone other than the right-holder exercises his power to strip the right-holder of his right. Inalienable rights cannot be lost in any of these ways. Nonetheless, renunciation is fundamental, and rights that cannot be renounced are inalienable.

If a right cannot be renounced, it is either because the right-holder cannot be without it or because the right brings about some insupportable evil when loosed from any right-holder. Since rights are impotent unless wielded by right-holders, a free-floating right could only be intolerably bad if it were a right that someone must exercise to avert evil, in other words, a right to perform an essential duty. Of course, persons cannot renounce their rights to perform any of their duties on a whim, but rights to perform many duties are in principle renounceable. If a person has a duty that conflicts with someone else's more urgent duty, he may renounce his right to fulfill his duty in deference to the other person's heavier moral burden. Only rights permitting duties so critical that they invariably take precedence are impossible to renounce because of the indefeasibility of these duties.

There seems to be no cogent basis, however, for granting that there are duties which can never be superseded. Since duties and the rights to do them may be more or less compelling depending on circumstances, the supposition that they are arrayed on a fixed hierarchy indicating their importance is misguided. Furthermore, if any absolute rights or duties straightforwardly stated how agents should act in all the multifarious circumstances that can arise, the rules specifying them would be so complex that human agents could not remember and apply them.

Still, someone might suggest that, despite the variable relations among most moral considerations, a single ultimate duty could dominate all the others. Unfortunately, there is no consensus about which duty is preeminent. Is it the principle of utility, the categorical imperative, or some as yet unimagined directive? Regardless of which it might be and whether everyone might eventually become convinced of its paramount stature, its absoluteness would remain problematic from the standpoint of its implementation. For moral agents will inevitably differ over what it requires of them. Lacking a decisive method for selecting the correct interpretation of their ultimate principle in the midst of controversy, opponents may never agree about whom their absolute principle authorizes to proceed and may be obliged to resolve their differences by substituting an extraneous decision procedure, such as voting or taking turns. In practice, then, no plausible ultimate principle gives agents sufficiently unequivocal guidance to obviate moral disputes and thus to rule out reliance on subsidiary principles.[8] Whether or not an omniscient moral thinker could identify an absolute moral precept and could discern each of its prescriptions for action, people cannot achieve perfect moral insight.

In view of this limitation, the set of rights that cannot be renounced because they entitle persons to perform essential duties can be presumed to be null. Accordingly, nonrenounceability can be understood exclusively as a relation, which is not mediated by duties to others, linking right-holders and certain of their rights; and human rights can be understood—as traditionally they have been understood—as rights aimed primarily at protecting right-holders through the guarantees they afford.

Once it has been established that nonrenounceable rights are characterized as such solely because they are necessary to right-holders, it is possible to show that these rights cannot be conditionally waived or transferred for the same reason that they cannot be renounced. Rights that are inseparable from right-holders are not temporarily separable from them or separable from them provided that a suitable recipient can be found. For it is not the permanence of the separation or the undesirability of stray rights that precludes renunciation. It is the impossibility of the separation itself.

Usually it makes a difference whether a right is forsworn permanently or temporarily and whether it is simply forsworn or turned over to someone else. Of course, if a person can predict accurately that no occasion to exercise his right will arise during the period for which he has waived it while acknowledging that at some other time he could desperately need to assert it, he can safely waive it temporarily. However, in that case, the right-holder's waiver would be an empty gesture which should not count as an effective conditional waiver. Under somewhat less propitious circumstances, a right-holder may reckon that the losses he is apt to sustain within the time frame of his waiver would be absorbable or recoverable though the losses resulting from unrestricted renunciation would be unendurable. Similarly, a right-holder who cedes his right to some chosen individual can to some extent protect himself by cautiously picking a friendly recipient for his right. The question is whether nonrenounceable rights can be conditionally waived or transferred on either of the contemplated types of gamble.

Underlying the suggestion that nonrenounceable rights might yet be waivable or transferable is the supposition that the obstacle to renunciation of a nonrenounceable right is the enormity and inevitability of the harm renunciation would inflict on the right-holder. If the harm could be avoided or its horror mitigated, the right could be renounced. Since calculated conditional waiver and transfer reduce the degree of harm and its likelihood to acceptable dimensions, the argument concludes, nonrenounceable rights can be conditionally waived and transferred.

Though initially plausible, this argument rests on a flawed analysis of nonrenounceable rights. A right-holder can lose any right without necessarily suffering any harm. Once bereft of a right, a person is morally liable to harms that he formerly was not, but other people may never elect to take advantage of his moral defenselessness.[9] In short, bad consequences cannot be invoked to account for nonrenounceability because none may occur.

Other prospective accounts of nonrenounceability are less receptive to conditional waiver and transfer. Either the mere liability to some harms is unbearable, and therefore rights protecting persons from these harms are not renounceable, or some entitlements are indissoluble, and therefore rights conferring them defy renunciation. The first of these accounts is less appealing than the second because it suggests that nonrenounceable rights make right-holders morally immune to some harms, which they could only do if they were absolute. But the important point to notice is that both of these accounts of nonrenounceability entail that nonrenounceable rights are nonwaivable and nontransferable, as well. If liability to a harm is itself intolerable, any risk of the harm will be too great. And if an entitlement is inextricable from right-holders, the corresponding right cannot be briefly nullified or permanently reassigned. Nonrenounceable rights, in other words, obviate estimates of the costs and benefits of projected conditional waivers and transfers.

Yet, someone might complain that rights ordinarily classed among human rights are commonly transferred to a guardian when a right-holder succumbs to an ailment that renders him incompetent. Indeed, if human rights were nontransferable, it might be argued, comatose or insane right-holders would be effectively without rights. While it is undeniable that a guardian can assume responsibility for an incapacitated individual's welfare, it is not clear that this custodial role presupposes a transfer of the ward's rights. Ordinarily, right-holders can exercise their rights in various ways, including sacrificing the goods conferred by their rights to a cause they believe worthy and forgiving abridgments of their rights as they are moved to do so. In contrast, a guardian must adopt a conservative policy in regard to her ward's interests; that is, a guardian must assume that the ward would want to get and keep the objects of her rights and must endeavor to secure this end on her behalf. Guardians are rarely justified in acting on the assumption that a ward's principles or emotional ties would have swayed her to sacrifice the object of a right or to forgive an abridgment. But what shows conclusively that the guardian-ward relationship involves no rights transfer is that guardians are enjoined never to subordinate their protection of their wards to purposes, such as scientific experimentation or political change, which they, but not their wards, hold dear. A guardian serves as a proxy in exercising her ward's rights but does not have the same latitude in exercising these rights as she would have if the rights had been transferred.

Still, the contention that all nonrenounceable rights are also nonwaivable and nontransferable could be admitted without conceding that all nonrenounceable rights are inalienable. It might prove possible for nonrenounceable rights to be forfeited or revoked, and these forfeitable or revocable rights would be alienable.

A right-holder forfeits a right when he no longer meets the qualifications for the right, and a right can be revoked if someone other than the right-holder has the authority to take away his right. Frequently, persons forfeit rights involuntarily, for example, by forgetting renewal procedures or by falling ill at inopportune moments. But persons may take advantage of regulations stating qualifications for rights to forfeit them deliberately, for example, by letting deadlines pass or by avoiding required appearances. Similarly, though rights are often revoked unexpectedly, a right-holder may instigate revocation of his rights. Provided that right-holders can opt to forfeit their rights and can elicit revocation of them, their rights are renounceable since intentional forfeiture or deliberately provoked revocation is nothing other than indirect renunciation.

Of course, it is possible for a person to know that the penalty for doing a certain act is forfeiture and yet to do the act deliberately but without intending to forefeit the right (at most, intending to risk forfeiture). Such an individual is not willfully forfeiting his right and therefore cannot be accused of indirectly renouncing it. Nevertheless, if the qualifications for a right allow right-holders who are so inclined to renounce this right indirectly, it is a renounceable right, though many cases of forfeiture are not also cases of renunciation. Once a right has been shown to be nonrenounceable, it follows that it must be immune to optional forfeiture and revocation, too. Nonrenounceable rights, then, can only be forfeitable or revocable if the circumstances triggering forfeiture or revocation are beyond the control of right-holders.

Forfeiture and revocation could be governed by rules contrived to prevent right-holders from manipulating them in order to renounce their rights. However, thus removing the qualifications for human rights and the grounds for revoking them from the control of right-holders would have two unacceptable consequences. First, it would be impossible on any but arbitrary bases to distinguish considerations that justify abridging a right from ones that render the right forfeit or subject to revocation. Only when a right-holder abuses a human right does forfeiture or revocation, as opposed to abridgment, seem at all warranted. But if the right-holder's misuse of his right is the sole way that he can lose it, he will be able to choose this course as a means of renouncing his right. Second, enforced forfeiture or revocation of rights for reasons beyond the right-holder's control would be paradoxical in light of the supposition that these rights are so integral to right-holders that they cannot be renounced regardless of how compelling or noble the right-holder's reasons may be. Surely, what can be taken from a person for a good reason he can relinquish for the same reason, and what he cannot relinquish for any reason cannot legitimately be taken from him.

A demonstration that a right is nonrenounceable, then, suffices to show that it is inalienable. Still, it is not obvious how to argue that a right is impossible to renounce. While the strategy of sifting through situations checking for intuitions disconfirming the nonrenounceability of candidate rights cannot be avoided entirely, this approach is too cumbersome and inconclusive unless criteria for nonrenounceability are available to guide the selection of situations to explore and, also, to orient intuitive responses to the ones chosen as test cases.

4. Sources of Criteria for Inalienable Rights

To justify the claim that there are inalienable rights, it must be shown that some rights establish between prospective right-holders and a good a relation which these individuals cannot disrupt. For example, if persons had an inalienable right to have dessert with lunch, it would be because persons could not dispense with the control over their lives which this right would afford, namely, the opportunity to finish lunch with a sweet. Of course, this right seems an unlikely candidate for inalienability because dessert with lunch is a luxury that is probably harmful to most persons and because no urgent reason to guarantee persons the option of eating dessert with lunch readily comes to mind. An adequate defense of an inalienable right must make up these failings. It must give an account of the bond between the right and the right-holder and an explanation of the moral impregnability of that bond.

The ties between individuals and inalienable rights have been analyzed as consequences of psychological theories, concepts of personhood, and social ideals. A psychological account urges that the laws of psychology preclude any right-holder's relinquishing the options which are secured by inalienable rights.[10] An account derived from the concept of a person contends that these options are necessary conditions for personhood or some related desideratum.[11] And an account predicated on a social ideal holds that a social ideal cannot be achieved unless persons enjoy certain options.[12] Each type of account identifies some property or properties that right-holders share—these may include interests, needs, capabilities, and vulnerabilities—and argues that the guarantees of rights answering to these properties are, for reasons of psychology, the idea of a person, or the goal of social perfection, inseparable from right-holders.

Implicit in each of these kinds of account is a position regarding the moral ratification of the ties between inalienable rights and the individuals who possess them. If there are any rights that are psychologically impossible to give up, it would be futile for a moral system to permit or require their renunciation. Alternatively, if some concept of the person is correct and implies possession of a set of rights, any moral system that accommodates alienation of these rights would condone extinguishing personhood. Finally, an ostensible social ideal which cannot be realized unless all persons have a designated set of rights must be exposed as a false or unimportant one before moral systems can with impunity allow agents to give up the rights the ideal presupposes. Clearly, any list of inalienable rights defended in one of these ways will be as credible as the psychology, concept of personhood, or social teleology on which it depends.

Still, among accounts of inalienable rights that appear equally plausible, there may be a telling difference. Though all theories of inalienable rights contend that moral systems *should* not allow individuals to part with certain rights, few have gone so far as to affirm that moral systems *cannot* allow this partition. Theories based on a concept of the person or on a

The Problem of Natural Rights

social ideal point out that severing persons from the rights they identify as inalienable would have consequences which would be deemed undesirable by any moral position incorporating the concept of the person or the social ideal which generates the set of inalienable rights. But they do not proceed to show that these consequences are inadmissible from the standpoint of any acceptable moral system. Without this final step, the tie between inalienable rights and right-holders is attenuated, for it may be negated by some tenable moral code.

Psychological theories are more ambitious than their conceptual and idealistic counterparts inasmuch as they produce a psychological law which, it is claimed, would obstruct any sane individual's attempt to renounce certain rights. These theories thus declare that morality is powerless in the face of ineluctable psychological truths. Inalienability is a natural fact which moral systems must codify by forbidding persons to accept apparent renunciations as valid. Unfortunately, the weakness of these theories, which lies in the dubiety of their purported psychological truths, seems to be incurable. The astonishing diversity of human conduct belies the claim that any acts, including all forms of rights renunciation, are psychologically impossible.

Happily, the psychological approach to the problem of inalienable rights does not exhaust the possible ways of showing that there are some rights which morality cannot allow persons to alienate. The concept of a moral system is also the source of an argument to this effect. If the question is 'Why are certain rights inalienable?' a promising reply is that no satisfactory moral system can allow persons to renounce these rights. In other words, whatever the content of a moral system's general principles and whatever the substance of its situation-specific prescriptions, proscriptions, and permissions, it cannot countenance alienation of certain rights and remain an acceptable moral system.

The suggestion that inalienable rights be derived from the idea of a satisfactory moral system presupposes criteria of adequacy which moral systems must satisfy, such as consistency and applicability, but which need not together pick out one and only one satisfactory code of conduct. Should several moral systems prove to meet all pertinent criteria of adequacy, further argument will be needed to assess whether one of them is superior to the others. However, the purpose of introducing the concept of an adequate moral system in the present context is solely to examine its implications with respect to rights.

In order to highlight criteria of adequacy that bear directly on inalienable rights, it is necessary to explicate rights renunciation and then to consider how the concept of moral agency constrains moral systems. After all, it is moral agents who cannot renounce inalienable rights. Now, if there are criteria of adequacy which moral systems must meet before moral agents can be held responsible for adhering to their directives, and if these criteria of adequacy implicitly debar moral systems from allowing renunciation of some rights, these rights must be inalienable.[13] The role of inalienable rights in adequate moral systems, on this view, is to legitimate the practical demands these conduct codes make on persons.

Several reasons recommend basing a theory of inalienable rights on the concept of an adequate moral system. First, criteria of adequacy for moral systems lend themselves to persuasive defense and have no immediate connection with the controversy swirling around inalienable rights. Thus, broad consensus about a theory of inalienable rights built on this foundation is not inconceivable. Second, a theory of this kind can be expected to coordinate conceptual considerations with psychological and social ones. Since an adequate moral system must be addressed to human agents living together, it is hard to imagine how a conceptual argument deriving inalienable rights from the idea of an adequate moral system could fail to introduce elements of individual psychology and social idealism. Finally, this method cannot yield a merely conditional account of inalienable rights. Whereas theories based on a concept of personhood or on a social ideal have always allowed us to dispose of their normative conclusions by expunging the premised concept or ideal from our preferred moral system, we cannot deny inalienable rights deduced from the idea of an adequate moral system without rejecting the idea of morality.

The possibility that moral action consists of carrying out moment-to-moment or occasional imperatives vouchsafed by intuition might seem to undercut the method of analyzing and defending inalienable rights I propose to adopt. If these prescriptions are not reducible to any system, it would appear that a person could be moral without embracing any moral system and therefore that inalienable rights deduced from the idea of an adequate moral system could be denied without confounding morality. I set aside the highly implausible suggestion that moral intuition is completely independent of rules. But if the claim that the set of intuitive prescriptions cannot be comprehended by a moral system means that no manageable set of normative principles, operating rules, and factual propositions could capture the complexity and subtlety manifest in intuitive prescriptions, it presents no difficulty for my approach to inalienable rights.

Concurrence about inalienable rights requires neither selection of a single correct moral system nor full and determinate articulation of the moral systems containing these rights. Since agreement about which rights are inalienable is compatible with disagreement about the relative stringencies of these rights and about how these rights can be respected in diverse circumstances, introducing inalienable rights into a moral system need not exclude intuitive weighing of options in moral deliberation nor intuitive apprehension of moral solutions. There may be inalienable rights though there is no calculus controlling their implementation. Moreover, the same inalienable rights may be included in moral systems that differ in other respects. Because the stable content of inalienable rights consists of certification of a set of interests coupled with demarcation of a measure of autonomy vis-à-vis a good, but not the details of exercising and respecting these rights, inalienable rights can be accommodated by moral systems comprising disparate principles as well as employing divergent techniques of moral judgment.

Whereas any set of absolute rights would prejudge the proper handling of moral dilemmas involving the rights and would rule out moral systems capable of yielding contrary prescriptions, the primary impact of inalienable rights is their shaping of the moral sphere.[14] By according right-holders the status of participants in situations in which the objects of these rights are at stake, inalienable rights delineate a view of moral agents and their rightful concerns which structures moral interaction insofar as these concerns enter into it. Of course, inalienable rights are not normatively vacuous: they affirm that individuals are entitled to specified goods and, in the absence of decisive overriding considerations, ought to be granted these goods. Nevertheless, the latitude inalienable rights permit in effecting these entitlements and their emphasis on rights possession apart from rights respect compel us to register their salient contribution as the formal one of fixing a set of moral issues and the parties to them.

Searches for universal features of morality usually founder in the attempt to identify points of convergence among the precepts of different moral systems. Impeded initially by the paucity of candidates, this enterprise is hampered by a further difficulty about what is to count as a common element. Identically worded principles can appear in different contexts that skew their applications, and prescriptions exacting identical conduct can be arrived at for different reasons. Circumventing these problems, a theory of inalienable rights locates the universal element of morality, instead, in the conception of a group of agents engaged in moral relations.

Uncompromisingly at odds as moral systems may in some respects be, it should not be surprising that they share a core understanding of the structure of the moral universe. If they did not basically concur about who are moral agents and what are moral issues, they would not constitute alternative moral systems, for they would be addressed to altogether different sets of individuals whose moral preoccupations would not overlap. Though it is sometimes tempting to think that strident proponents of opposing moral practices do not inhabit the same moral world, their determination to convince their antagonists of their errors shows that they regard one another as moral agents confronting the same moral problems.[15] Moreover, occasional conversions suggest that this mutual acknowledgment is well founded. If criteria for inalienable rights can be derived from the idea of an adequate moral system and if some rights can be shown to satisfy these criteria, the resulting theory of inalienable rights would partially account for the possibility of moral argument among individuals holding antithetical moral views. And more important still, it would set limits on the profundity of intelligible moral discord. Whatever their differences, moral adversaries would be obliged to concede that they all have certain inalienable rights.

2

A Contribution of Inalienable Rights to the Adequacy of Moral Systems

The broad problem of analyzing the tie between inalienable rights and the individuals who possess them encompasses two subsidiary issues. One is the problem of specifying what is meant by saying that individuals cannot give up inalienable rights. The other is the problem of explaining this incapacity. In dealing with this pair of problems, I will concern myself solely with renunciation of rights since, as has been shown, what could be said about other forms of rights loss would depend on the outcome of an investigation of rights renunciation.[1]

1. Varieties of Rights Renunciation

Renunciation sunders the connection between the renouncer and the thing renounced. Since a moral right grants an individual prerogatives with respect to the disposition of the object of the right, renunciation of the right must morally divest the individual of his prerogatives. In order to accomplish this separation, the renouncer must release others from the obligation his right implies. A right entitles a person to enjoy some good if he so wishes, and it requires others not to interfere with the right-holder's enjoyment of that good or to supply it for him on demand. Once a person has renounced a right, others gain a liberty to do or not to do what they were formerly obligated to do or not. An inalienable right, then, grants the right-holder an entitlement which he cannot undo because he cannot grant others permission to abrogate the obligation his right imposes on them.

Morally permissible actions fall into three categories: 1) simple permissibility, 2) permissibility in virtue of occupying a position or meeting a qualification, and 3) permissibility in virtue of a compelling moral reason. Conduct which is simply permissible is conduct that no one is empowered to regulate and which is in no way wrong. Though a person's obligations may consume his time and keep him from engaging in activities that are simply permissible, countless activities, ranging from daydreaming to mathematical speculation, are simply permissible. A second class of permissions consists of activities which are wrong unless the agent occupies the requisite position or meets the specified qualification. As a result of the special relationship between parents and their children, parents are authorized to raise their offspring as they see fit, and strangers are barred from meddling in this process. Similarly, the recipient of a promise is permitted to make demands on the promisor which would be indecent, if not immoral, in the absence of the promisor's prior express commitment. The third type of permission comprises actions which are morally wrong—either wrong in themselves or wrong in view of special arrangements—but which compelling moral considerations to the contrary can render permissible. Whereas to lie is ordinarily to violate a moral proscription, lying in order to save a life is morally permissible. Likewise, parental delinquency can occasion the reassignment of child-rearing responsibilities and prerogatives. Since all obligations are prima facie obligations, there is no action that cannot in principle be permissible in virtue of a compelling moral reason.[2]

Contribution of Inalienable Rights 25

Any right that authorizes the right-holder to control conduct that could be simply permissible can be renounced. Whereas a right-holder can use the device of a conditional waiver to restrict his permission to situations in which a good moral reason calls for acting on it, or he can use the device of a transfer to assign his permission to another individual or collectivity, a right-holder's renunciation issues a simple permission. In unreservedly disavowing a right, a person removes whatever moral stigma would otherwise attach to failure to comply with the right's correlative obligation and frees others to embark upon this formerly forbidden course.

The various measures available to a hereditary monarch who wishes to abdicate illustrate these possibilities. She may waive her sovereign rights on condition that democratic institutions be established and maintained. If the populace then declares fealty to a foreign monarch, the waiver is void, and royal powers rightfully revert to the original queen. Alternatively, she may transfer her sovereign rights to a previously elected legislative body. If the transfer does not stipulate that this body must retain sovereign authority, this legislature would be free to rule indefinitely or to set up a new royal line. Finally, the queen could renounce her sovereignty. As distinguished from conditional waiver and transfer, renunciation places no constraints whatsoever on the disposition of the object of the renounced right. Through renunciation, the queen would shun all of the prerogatives of her hereditary crown. She would neither use her sovereign rights to pass them along to a designated successor, nor would she retain any residual hereditary rights in the event that she deplored subsequent developments. Whereas her subjects had been obligated to acquiesce in her governance and foreign powers had been obligated not to intervene in her handling of domestic matters (assuming the legitimacy of hereditary monarchy), the queen's renunciation would transform her into a citizen and would leave a political vacuum which anyone would be at liberty to try to fill. Renunciation creates a simple permission.

Yet, when seen from the perspective of the renouncer, renunciations are not all alike since the circumstances precipitating renunciation vary widely. Schematically, right-renouncers may act on impulse, out of passion, out of self-interest, or for moral reasons. These grounds for renunciation are neither exhaustive nor mutually exclusive. Nevertheless, renunciations based purely upon caprice, ardent feeling, or prudence differ from those dictated by compelling moral considerations in an important respect. The former which I shall group under the heading 'renunciation by fiat' leave the right-renouncer as free with respect to the object of the renounced right as everyone else is. In contrast, persons whose moral convictions oblige them to renounce a right—I shall call these undertakings 'conscientious renunciations'—must assume an obligation of self-restraint with respect to the object of the right that is commensurate with the reason for the renunciation. Not to do so would be to negate the renunciation in a morally unacceptable fashion.

That renunciation of a right generates such an obligation is plain where a Hohfeldian liberty is at stake.[3] In order to renounce a liberty, a person must assume a duty not to do what he was formerly entitled to do, thus freeing others to do it without interference from him. But Hohfeld contends that renunciation of a claim right merely converts this right into a no-right, and it is not immediately clear that this conversion ever commits the renouncer to any special duty of self-restraint. Since possession of a no-right with respect to some good is compatible with possession of a liberty with respect to the same good, it seems that the renouncer of a claim right may open competition over the object of his right and number himself among the competitors. He would not, then, be morally bound to let others dispose of the object of his right.

Some instances of renunciation by fiat plainly warrant the contention that renunciation need not sever the renouncer from all prerogatives with respect to the object of the right he shuns. A millionaire oil magnate with a penchant for rugged competition might renounce her right to a rich oil field solely in order to join in the ensuing struggle over it. She may lose the contest, in which case her liberty is canceled and she is

Contribution of Inalienable Rights   27

obligated to honor the new owner's property right, or she may win, in which case she regains her exclusive claim right and others' liberties are canceled. Nonetheless, for the duration of the game, she has both a no-right and a liberty, and her participation does not contradict her renunciation.

Still, the cases of renunciation by fiat that allow the renouncer to exercise a liberty with respect to the object of the renounced right should not seduce us into overlooking cases of renunciation by fiat in which retention of a liberty is suspect. Suppose, as a token of her esteem, the scion of a wealthy family solemnly promises a Marxist friend to donate her inherited fortune to the cause of her friend's choice at any time she requests it. After awhile, the Marxist capriciously renounces her right to exact this contribution, but, having released the promisor from her bond, she promptly begins trying to inveigle the contribution from her. One explanation of the renouncer's behavior might be that anyone is free to try to induce anyone else who will listen to undertake any course of action that is not immoral. Unless the renouncer has disavowed this sweeping liberty as well, her pleadings are perfectly in order. Be this as it may, the promisor would be right to be troubled by the turn of events, for it calls the renunciation into question. Did the promisee realize that she was nullifying this particular claim on her benefactor's loyalties? Did she really mean to free this person to refuse to make the specified sacrifice? Of course, it is possible that the promisor could satisfy herself that the renunciation was valid and that her friend was now merely deploying a background liberty. Perhaps, she wanted to know whether the promisor would do her bidding simply out of friendship or only because she had promised. Still, the renouncer's trifling with her wealthy friend's feelings in this way manifests a devious distrustfulness out of keeping with friendship. In regard to some renunciations by fiat, then, to exercise a liberty with respect to the object of the right impugns the renouncer's character if it does not compromise the renunciation.

Although renunciation by fiat is formally compatible with a competitive liberty held by the renouncer, the intricacies of human interaction frequently condemn this constellation of moral prerogatives. Only insofar as competitive maneuvering with respect to the object of a right does not confute renunciation of the right is it possible for a right-holder to renounce a right to a good without ceding his liberty with respect to it. Renunciation by fiat does not preclude the renouncer's pursuing the benefit his erstwhile right confers because this form of renunciation does not imply a favorable assessment of others' exercising the simple permission that renunciation issues. Conscientious renunciation, however, presents a more complicated picture.

2. Conscientious Renunciation

To renounce a right conscientiously, the right-holder not only must recognize that there are compelling grounds to deny his right but also must not object to others' acting on these reasons. If he does not acknowledge any compelling moral reason for extinguishing his right, he cannot conscientiously renounce it. To reach the conclusion that circumstances require him to allow others not to recognize his right, the right-holder must discover reasons to approve of this departure. Unless such reasons present themselves, there would be no moral grounds to make this course available to anyone. Through conscientious renunciation, then, a right-holder voices his assent to others' nullification of his right. Since subsequent resistance to others' use of this new option would negate this implicit approbation, but since conscientious renunciation is impossible without it, a liberty to oppose conduct that would have violated the renounced right could not be exercised without contradicting the terms of the renunciation. Such a liberty would be morally otiose. Thus, conscientious renunciation requires that the right-holder assume an obligation to let others dispose of the object of his right.

Now, the claim that the renouncer's reasons for disavowing his right determine whether or not his renunciation restricts his liberty with respect to the object of his right might seem to strain human discernment too much. Since fathoming our own reasons is often difficult and since others' reasons are even less transparent, basing this obligation of self-restraint solely on the renouncer's reasons may obfuscate matters unduly. Although it is undeniable that obligations predicated on observable incidents are easier to ascribe to agents, it is also undeniable that obligations commonly depend on our own or others' reasons. If out of generosity and attentiveness to an acquaintance's needs one person gives another a timely gift, the recipient owes her benefactor gratitude; if instead, her acquaintance offers to help her because she can take a sizable tax deduction for this gift, gratitude on the recipient's part would be out of place. Similarly, conscientious objectors accept moral liabilities that draft resisters refuse. Frequently, persons must rely on uncertain insight into motives and reasons to assess their moral responsibilities. Accordingly, the moral significance of the division between renunciation by fiat and conscientious renunciation makes no extraordinary demands on our perspicacity.

Nevertheless, this dichotomy might be questioned on the grounds that a renouncer can exercise a competitive liberty to contradict frivolous or self-interested reasons for renunciation in the same way that he can contradict moral reasons for relinquishing a right by availing himself of this option. An American gourmande who renounces her citizenship rights in order to reside permanently in France becomes an expatriate by fiat. Yet, if she subsequently exercises her competitive liberty to try to immigrate back to the culinary wasteland she has forsaken, her action constitutes a rejection of her original reason for her renunciation. Why is she not bound by this reason while an exile from a tyrannical regime who has conscientiously renounced her citizenship in protest is bound by hers?

Three features of conscientious renunciation soften the impact of this query somewhat. First, the conscientious right-renouncer could continue to possess other rights that to some extent overlap her citizenship rights and duplicate their content. If so, her obligation of self-restraint would not extend to declining to assert and benefit from these additional rights until such time as they, too, were extinguished. Conscientious renunciation can be piecemeal. Second, the conscientious right-renouncer could later realize that her ideal would be better served by returning to struggle against the entrenched political system. Moral agents can discover that they have made mistakes, and conscientious renunciation does not prohibit anyone from trying to rectify a misjudgment. Third, if the tyrannical regime were overthrown, the right-renouncer might properly seek repatriation in order to help build a more just society. Circumstances can change so markedly (not to mention, unexpectedly) that the reasons for conscientious renunciation cease to constrain the renouncer's exercise of background liberties. Like all other obligations, the obligation of self-restraint that conscientious renunciation creates is a prima facie obligation that may be overridden and that may diminish in force. It is neither absolute nor final.

Yet, conscientious renunciation and renunciation by fiat are asymmetrical inasmuch as the former generates a prima facie obligation of self-restraint which the latter does not. But this difference holds no mystery, for it is straightforwardly attributable to the different reasons for these two types of undertaking. To affirm compelling moral reasons to act in a particular manner is to affirm that it would be wrong not to do so unless countervailing considerations emerge. Arbitrary inconsistency in such matters is morally culpable. But, of course, no blame attaches to inconstancy in the prosecution of nonmoral purposes like amusement or gain. As a result, it is obligatory to refrain from confounding a conscientious renunciation, whereas it is permissible to confound any renunciation by fiat.

Still, some bona fide conscientious renunciations seem to defeat this conclusion since it is possible to have a good moral reason for initiating a competition over the object of a right. The heir to a vast fortune, for instance, might become convinced that unearned wealth is unjustified and, for that reason, renounce her inheritance. In renouncing these amassed property rights, the argument continues, this individual authorizes others to endeavor to gain possession of her erstwhile holdings but does not bar herself from doing the same thing. She, too, may work to acquire these goods in competition with others.

While the conclusion of this argument is correct, it misses the point of the claim that a conscientious right-renouncer incurs an obligation of self-restraint with respect to the object of his former right. The heir depicted in the example does not ascetically renounce all worldly possessions. Rather, she renounces only her inherited wealth because she believes that owners ought to have done something to deserve their property. Clearly, the terms of this conscientious renunciation do not leave the renouncer bereft of any property she has already earned. Furthermore, they afford her the option of trying to earn back the holdings constituting her inheritance though they deprive her of the option of asserting a hereditary claim. If an aunt sues to prevent the dissolution of the fortune, the renouncer cannot counter by standing on her ancestral rights. The precise lineaments of the obligation of self-restraint conscientious renunciation engenders depend on the reason for the renunciation. Unless the grounds for conscientious renunciation are such that the renouncer must forswear all further truck with the object of a spurned right, conscientious renunciation does not void all of the renouncer's background liberties regarding this good.

Another way to see why conscientious renunciation must impose an obligation of self-restraint on the renouncer is to consider how this mode of renunciation can be efficacious at all. Since no right is absolute, any right can be abridged in virtue of a superseding moral consideration, regardless of whether the right-holder consents. Thus, conscientious renunciation is not a necessary condition for permissibility in virtue of a compelling moral reason (nor, for that matter, is conscientious conditional waiver or conscientious transfer). If conscientious renunciation is not to be relegated to the status of an empty formality in these situations, it must change the right-holder's position in some way that permissibility in virtue of a compelling moral reason, taken alone, does not. A right-holder whose right is subject to infringement is permitted to oppose this measure and to demand recognition as a victim if his claims are not honored.[4] Either conscientious renunciation is superfluous, or it deprives the right-holder of these options by creating for him an obligation to submit impassively to treatment his right would have permitted him to resist.

At this juncture, it might be conceded that a right-holder must assume an obligation of self-restraint in order to renounce a right that others could permissibly abridge without his concurrence. Still, against my position, it could be urged that a right-holder could retain a competitive liberty in renouncing a right which others could not permissibly abridge unless he had consented or unless his consent were annexed to a moral reason. When no independent warrant for abridging a right obtains or the justification for abridging a right is inconclusive or controversial, failure to obtain the right-holder's agreement before abridgment violates his right. In circumstances of this sort, the right-holder's renunciation would radically alter the moral situation by transforming a rights violation into a fully justified action. Accordingly, this renunciation cannot be dismissed as nugatory, and the right-holder's assuming an obligation to acquiesce in this reversal can be regarded as a further, perhaps excessive, cooperative step.

The defect of this account of conscientious renunciation is that it neglects to explain how compelling moral reasons figure in the renunciation. This omission is not surprising since conscientious renunciation is not necessarily involved in situations in which abridgment would be impermissible without the right-holder's consent. Renunciation by fiat would suffice. Only if the renouncer embraces moral reasons for eschewing his right does he incur an obligation not to resist the uses to which others may put the benefit his right confers.

A tale adapted from Grimm may help to make the distinctive force of conscientious renunciation more vivid.[5] To find a wife worthy of his wondrous son, the king sets a twofold test: as a proof of her valor, the suitor must win a race against the king's wind-fleet runner, and, as a proof of her devotion to the prince, she must consent to be executed if she is defeated. Let us accept the chivalric morality of the story and grant that renouncing one's right to life can be morally justified as a means of testifying to one's affection. Now suppose that a suitor appears, challenges the king's runner, declares her title to live void if she is defeated on the racecourse, and loses the contest. She has irretrievably lost the prince's hand. Nevertheless, her adoration for him remains intact as her having spurned her right to life demonstrates. Or does it? Surely, if she marches bravely to the gallows proclaiming that her life is worthless without the prince, her behavior does express the steadfastness of her commitment to the reason for her renunciation, that is, her unabated love. But, if instead she escapes from prison and sends a message to the court proclaiming her liberty to fight for her life, the king can reasonably conclude that this suitor's love for the prince did not last if it ever existed. A Hohfeldian adventuress who slyly retains a liberty of self-defense exhibits fickle, if not feigned, affections. In reserving this liberty, she makes ready to belie her reason for renouncing her right; in exercising it, she discredits her sincerity unless circumstances have changed in morally relevant ways or countervailing reasons have come to light.

Conscientious renunciation must be differentiated from renunciation by fiat as well as from rights possession despite good reason to renounce. Conscientious renunciation completely preempts the right-holder's prerogatives with respect to the benefit the reason picks out. Not only must the renouncer cease to be entitled to demand that others supply or not interfere with his enjoyment of the object of his right, but he must also cease to be entitled to try to keep this good and to try to prevent interference with his enjoyment of it. Renouncing a right for a moral reason affirms the undesirability of the right-holder's control over a certain good. It therefore commits the renouncer to making it morally possible for others to exercise control over the object of the right; making it morally possible for them to try to wrest control over this good from him does not suffice. Having conscientiously renounced a right, a person is morally vulnerable to treatment that the right forbade and is prima facie prohibited from defending himself against these harms. In sum, the presumption established by a right in support of a right-holder's resistance to abridgments is supplanted through conscientious renunciation by a presumption on the side of submission to comparable misusage. It is the difference between agreeing to disagree and recanting one's beliefs, the difference between reducing one's prerogatives by fiat and altogether disavowing them conscientiously.

It would be impossible to renounce a right conscientiously if the person who possesses the right could never be obligated to tolerate the disposition others might make of the object of the right. Despite the extra burden conscientious renunciation, as distinct from renunciation by fiat, imposes on the renouncer, the conjecture that the most important rights are conscientiously renounceable if they are renounceable at all is a plausible one. For it seems unlikely that persons could disavow such vital rights unless competing moral considerations mandated it. Thus, for this chapter and the next, I shall confine my treatment of inalienability to conscientious renunciation. Nevertheless, the possibility that rights which are not renounceable for reasons of conscience might yet be renounceable by fiat must be confronted; in chapter 5, I shall urge that the same rights that cannot be conscientiously renounced also cannot be renounced by fiat. Provisionally, however, I take an inalienable right to be a right that a person cannot renounce conscientiously because he cannot obligate himself to allow others to abridge it.

3. Obligation, Supererogation, and Rights

The preceding account of the inability of right-holders conscientiously to renounce inalienable rights raises a further question as to why it might be impossible to become obligated to suffer certain types of treatment and, in particular, to allow others to determine how to use the objects of certain rights. Usually these limitations are viewed as consequences of the extraordinary and acute importance of the objects associated with these rights; yet it is not at all obvious how the intuitive notion of extraordinary and acute importance can be made sufficiently precise to serve as a criterion for identifying inalienable rights. I propose to use the concept of supererogation to explicate the concept of a right that cannot be conscientiously renounced because of the surpassing value of its object.

The reason no one can become obligated to allow abridgments of inalienable rights is that these rights have objects that it is supererogatory whenever appropriate, and therefore never obligatory, to sacrifice altruistically.[6] Doing a supererogatory action involves a person's sacrificing something valuable to which he is entitled for someone else's benefit though he is not duty-bound to do so. Altruistic self-sacrifice exceeding the requirements of duty is the core of supererogation. Allowing someone to act in a way that would have violated a right if the right had not been renounced is equivalent to sacrificing the object of the right—temporarily or permanently—to someone else's purposes. Consequently, any right with an object that cannot properly be sacrificed for the benefit of others except supererogatorily will bar generation of an obligation to submit to abridgments of the right and will therefore bar renunciation of the right.

Anything to which a person has a right could in principle be sacrificed supererogatorily; however, the objects of a person's various rights can be graded with respect to their potential as supererogatory sacrifices. Some of our rights entitle us to goods that it would rarely be supererogatory to relinquish, such as a right to a penny or a right to a rubber band. Because these things are so easily acquired and because we generally place such a low value on them, only extraordinary circumstances—ones in which a person has an urgent and immediate need for her penny or rubber band—could elevate her giving them up for someone else's benefit to the class of supererogatory actions.

Other rights entitle us to goods that we are ordinarily not obliged to relinquish for the sake of other people but nevertheless may be obliged to relinquish for their sake. Though a person justifiably places a high value on something to which he is entitled, circumstances may yet determine whether or not his sacrifice of it is supererogatory or morally required. For example, it would ordinarily be supererogatory for a person to offer hospitality to homeless strangers, but it would not be supererogatory for her to provide shelter for strangers stranded by a blizzard in a desolate area. Although this person is entitled to the privacy of her home, the desperate need of another person for shelter may take precedence over the former's right. Thus a beneficiary's urgent need can reduce to an obligation an action that would usually be supererogatory.

Supererogation is commonly relative to circumstances. Circumstances can augment the value a thing has for the person who is entitled to it, and circumstances can create needs in other people that are sufficiently pressing to supersede a person's entitlement. Thus, whether an altruistic sacrifice is obligatory or supererogatory will frequently depend on the context in which the action is done. Still, there remains a problem about limiting cases of supererogation.

One end of the spectrum is sealed off by the lower limit on the class of things that can be made the objects of rights. The concept of a right precludes the possibility of rights which entitle persons to things which could not conceivably be sacrificed supererogatorily. A right that gave a person discretion over something which he could not under any circumstances need would be pointless and consequently too feeble to impose any obligation on others to respect it. It makes nonsense of the concept of a right to say there can be rights which no one is ever obligated to respect. The other end of the spectrum is much more interesting. It raises the question of what could render an entitlement impervious to circumstances, that is, not amenable to obligatory sacrifice.

An altruistic sacrifice that is supererogatory whenever appropriate would occupy an odd position in the moral universe. Such a sacrifice would be permissible but never required, and it would evoke praise but not emulation. Why, it must be asked, are moral systems obliged to adopt this circumspect view of certain kinds of action? In what follows, I shall argue that no moral system can require its adherents to destroy moral agents because a moral system capable of generating an obligation to destroy these individuals would be self-defeating. Then I shall show how this limitation on the content of moral obligation bears on self-destruction, supererogation, and inalienable rights.

4. The Inadequacy of Self-defeating Moral Systems

A moral system is self-defeating if it holds both that moral agents ought to do their duty and that moral interaction as prescribed by the moral system ought to stop. A self-defeating moral system is capable of halting moral interaction in at least one of two ways: 1) its own prescriptions necessitate adoption of some competing moral system, for example, by bringing about conditions in which its own principles are no longer applicable, or 2) its prescriptions eventuate in circumstances that preclude further moral activity altogether, for example, by prescribing the destruction of all moral agents. From the standpoint of a moral system, general cessation of adherence to its principles constitutes an inadmissible evil. For, I shall argue, this outcome contravenes the metaprescription that moral agents ought to carry out the dictates of morality, which is itself an affirmation of the goodness of morality.

This metaprescription is an implementing element shared by all moral systems. Without it, moral systems would be devoid of practical efficacy. Utilitarians and Kantians alike must insist that moral agents, however they determine what the right action is, ought to do it since it is what morality requires of them. A deontologist would not be inclined to question this, yet a teleologist might hope to avoid this blunt imperative by appealing to an ultimate goal. But once a teleologist has urged that some simple or complex end is worthy of pursuit and has defined right action as action which promotes this end, his contention that persons ought to do actions for the sake of this end amounts to nothing more than the contention that persons ought to fulfill their obligations. Neither teleologists nor deontologists, it seems, can dispense with or improve upon the metaprescription requiring moral agents to do their duty since neither can subscribe to a supramoral goal for morality to serve.

Contrary to this, it has sometimes been maintained that the transcendent purpose of morality is to glorify a deity. Assuming this to be an intelligible aspiration, it must be incorporated into the moral systems it is supposed to transcend, since there would be no guarantee that morality will promote this end unless it is included among the professed goals of moral systems. Whether this exalted purpose can be integrated into moral systems depends on whether it can be made sufficiently determinate to support practical deliberation. However, when horrifying aims like cultivation of dysfunctional moral sentiments or annihilation of moral agents are proposed, the difficulties assume a different shape.[7] It is, perhaps, all too easy to imagine how such grim objectives could be achieved. Thus, the problem shifts from whether these goals could yield prescriptions for action to whether moral agents could be held responsible for carrying out the shocking prescriptions obtained.

A moral system and action guided by it must be regarded as good if moral agents are to be accountable for following its prescriptions. Though persons may sometimes knowingly pursue the bad, no one can be expected to devote himself deliberately and single-mindedly to the bad. Furthermore, if a moral system and the conduct it adjures are neither good nor evil, persons may unobjectionably opt to conform to it but could hardly be blamed for lapses in striving for indifference. Only when faced with a choice between neutrality and evil does neutrality appear sufficiently attractive to justify holding persons responsible for maintaining it. But should an opportunity to do good present itself, steadfast allegiance to

Contribution of Inalienable Rights 39

mediocrity would be perverse. Of course, moral systems need not be good throughout—sometimes sacrifices are mandatory, and sometimes nothing good can be achieved. But they must be good on the whole—general adherence must be good overall—before persons can be held responsible for upholding them. The question, then, is whether self-defeating objectives are compatible with regarding a moral system designed to serve them as good, or, in other words, whether these objectives are compatible with the metaprescription charging moral agents with responsibility for doing their duty.

Objectives involving termination of moral interaction as prescribed by a moral system can only be defended on the grounds that moral interaction in this, if not in all forms, is a blight. Either continued moral interaction is bad in itself, or it is worse than other possible outcomes. To evaluate the tenability of these contentions, it is necessary to consider three cases. One possibility is that of the reflexively self-condemnatory moral system, one that advocates cessation of obedience to its dictates on the grounds that following them is wicked. Another is the comparatively self-condemnatory moral system which represents a pair of possibilities. One version of this type of self-defeating moral system prefers elimination of the possibility of moral interaction to some greater evil, while the other prefers adoption of a superior way of ordering social intercourse.

The last of these three possibilities is easily dispatched since it is just a special case of the moral system that purports to serve a supramoral goal. A moral system that provides for its own replacement by a better regulatory mechanism must incorporate this end to ensure its subservience to attaining the desired result. In this case, the supplanting system and the moral system that gives way to it must be parts of a comprehensive moral system which either negotiates ascension through a succession of increasingly enlightened subsystems or orchestrates the interplay of an array of complementary subsystems. Notice, at this point, that neither of these heterogeneous moral systems would be self-defeating. Both allow for progress or adjustment to diverse circumstances without endorsing termination of adherence to their directives. Whatever the content of the subsystems, their implementation is not equivalent to suppression of the system that contains them, for the propriety of deploying any subsystem depends on the principles of the comprehensive system. Since the suggestion that a moral system might require itself to yield to another makes no sense unless the two systems are constituents of a unified whole which mediates their relations, no moral system can prescribe self-suppression in favor of an altogether distinct moral system.

Yet, a moral system could espouse a more severe kind of self-effacement in the form of a blanket condemnation of moral interaction. A moral system comprising this position would be committed not to the amelioration of interpersonal relations but rather to their cessation. However, in embracing this self-defeating objective and in declaring moral conduct to be bad, a moral system emasculates itself both as a means of perpetuating moral interaction and also as a means of terminating it. Once a moral system debases moral action, that is, conformity with its own prescriptions, it must exclude the metaprescription that moral agents ought to do their duty. Dutiful conduct is, after all, the target of the system's express contempt. Accordingly, no one would be bound to carry out the system's dictates, including its self-defeating program. By enunciating reflexive self-defeating goals, a moral system revokes its claim to be good and thereby negates its hold on its adherents' loyalties. Evidently, no moral system can embrace the metaprescription enjoining moral agents to comply with its dictates while denouncing moral action as bad in itself.

Still, it seems possible that a moral system could impose self-defeating measures under extreme circumstances without denouncing morality in general and therefore without blunting the metaprescription exacting fulfillment of its directives. For example, if all moral agents but one were to become incorrigibly evil and if this corruption were to be transmitted to all foreseeable generations, a moral system might require the remaining morally responsible individual to exterminate humanity rather than countenance unremitting evil. The persuasive force of this example stems from two sources: 1) exorcising evil falls squarely within the purview of morality, and 2) the choice between eternal evil and a moral void is not shadowed by doubts about whether good might eventually triumph. Nevertheless, the depicted situation and its remedial prescription are troubling because a horrifying act, mass killing, is required to bring about an uninspiring outcome, a depopulated, amoral social sphere.

Some conceivable situations are irredeemable. The one sketched above is a case in point, as is any situation in which a self-defeating prescription might reasonably be proposed. In these situations, an agent confronts a dilemma which pits the individual's scruples about how much responsibility he can shoulder against a devilish promise of alleviation. The individual is empowered to choose between performing a monstrous act capable of terminating a bad state of affairs and passively witnessing the persistence of the original dreadful state. The enormity of the deed and the awesomeness of the lingering evil are equipoised, while the change to be effected is neither a sufficient improvement nor inconsequential enough to tip the balance decisively.

This constellation of options and outcomes typifies situations in which a self-defeating obligation might be generated. The instigating situation must be an impasse manifesting evil in the highest degree. If any solution other than the demise of moral intercourse were feasible, a self-defeating prescription could not be contemplated; moreover, if maximal agony, depravity, or iniquity were not present, such an obligation could not possibly be warranted as a fitting remedy. What distinguishes an irremediable set of circumstances from other extremely grave situations is that the former locks individuals into a pernicious syndrome which they can only escape through self-destruction. And yet obliterating humanity is surely the most onerous of actions, an action which in virtue of its nature and its scale ordinarily counts as unsurpassably vile.

To surmise that a self-defeating action is obligatory is to reach the conclusion that extraordinary circumstances not only erase the wickedness of mass destruction but transmute it into righteousness. However, since no one occupies the viewpoint of eternity, no one is in a position to apprehend whether the destruction of all moral potential is ultimately better or worse than the persistence of rampant evil. Instead, agents must evaluate the immediate consequences of the available responses to the dilemma. Though the cessation of evil is generally an end worth pursuing, the appeal of this objective pales in the absence of beneficiaries. Similarly, the disruption of moral relations is normally an outcome to be deplored, yet the prospect of moral frustration unrelieved by moral satisfaction cancels much of the aversive power of this result. Because a self-defeating obligation mandates nothing more than the establishment of a moral vacuum—a state of affairs which in itself is neither good nor bad—and because rejecting this directive preserves moral consciousness though not moral adherence—a state of affairs which manifests the possibility of good while quashing its actualization—no moral system can certify a self-defeating obligation.

A self-defeating remedy would be a prescription no one could be held responsible for fulfilling. Since no accessible moral considerations conclusively sway deliberations about how to contend with tenacious and pervasive evil in favor of pitiable endurance or desperate revolt, no moral imperative applies under these conditions. A moral system that, nevertheless, generated one would create an optional duty. This duty, by confuting the metaprescription requiring moral agents to comply with moral prescriptions, would defeat the prescribing moral system in quotidian matters, as well. Thus, acceptable moral systems can require neither available course of action when extreme evil suggests a self-defeating release, and both alternatives must be permissible. Within the range of situations in which morality is competent, moral compliance must be recognizably good; but insofar as opaque circumstances bar discernment of the rationale supporting a moral imperative, moral codes can only refrain from gratuitously compounding the inevitable horror.

    An ambivalent moral system, holding a world empty of moral agents to be preferable if not ideal while countenancing continued moral interaction, might seem to evade my argument against self-defeating moral systems. Despite its misgivings about morality, this moral system could proscribe impairment and destruction of moral agency on the grounds that the distress resulting from prescribing extermination of moral agents would be far worse than the persistence of moral interaction. Such a moral system would incorporate a cataclysmic objective but also would be innocent of self-defeating prescriptions.

    The test of whether or not a moral system of this sort would count as self-defeating would be its prescription in a situation like the following: What should a person who has secretly invented a foolproof device for unexpectedly and painlessly vaporizing every moral agent do when the moral system's reasons for condemning moral interaction are apposite? On the one hand, the moral system could forbid mobilizing the envisioned device. In that case, we could infer that the moral system is not self-defeating inasmuch as its express approval of depopulation is practically impotent. An amoral ideal is not part of a moral system unless it functions as an objective which figures in the system's prescriptions. On the other hand, if there are circumstances in which the moral system's destructive ideal would take precedence and impose a duty to deploy the invention, the moral system is self-defeating. The triggering circumstances might be so remote that almost no one would be aware of the moral system's self-defeating potential, and in their ignorance persons might well adhere to the system as faithfully as they would if it were not self-defeating. Nevertheless, anyone who recognized the moral system's covert commitment to extinguishing moral interaction would have a conclusive reason to replace it with a moral system free of self-defeating objectives.

    Whatever a moral system's distinctive features, it

must function to guide conduct, and for this reason the metaprescription requiring moral agents to fulfill their obligations is ineliminable.[8] Despite its apparent innocuousness, this metaprescription exerts a substantial influence over the possible content of any moral system. Because it rules out obligations that persons could not be held responsible for fulfilling, it rules out obligations that imply the badness of moral compliance or the permissibility of noncompliance. Self-defeating obligations implicitly affirm either that moral interaction is bad absolutely or that it is worse than some other available option. If the former, the moral system authorizes its adherents to disregard any prescriptions it might generate. If the latter, the moral system obliges its adherents to suspend their belief in the preeminent goodness of ongoing moral intercourse and to accept on faith that termination of such relations is the better alternative. No more than they can be expected to devote their lives to the bad can persons be expected to dedicate themselves to the incomprehensible. Whether by simultaneously commanding and countermanding or by enforcing initiation into recondite moral mysteries, self-defeating moral systems perplex rational and conscientious agents.

5. Inadmissible Obligations

Moral systems can evince a self-defeating capability in various ways. However, the most blatant types of self-defeating moral systems specify circumstances under which someone would have a unilateral duty to destroy all moral agents or prescribe conduct which would produce the identical result if everyone were to incur the same duty simultaneously or cumulatively over time. The first of these forms need not detain us, but the second, which is more likely, poses a serious problem. For it would seem that a moral system could prescribe the destruction of moral agents with impunity provided that this duty were confined so as to preclude total extermination. Carefully formulated principles stipulating limits on destruction would make it possible for moral systems to prescribe any sort of conduct under some, though not all, circumstances. Hence there would be no type of action which could never be morally required and no type of altruistic self-sacrifice that would be supererogatory whenever appropiate and therefore no inalienable rights. If there are to be any inalienable rights, some self-destructive obligations must be inadmissible.

Rather than rehearsing grisly and fantastic situations in which destructive duties, however qualified, could conceivably be universalized, I shall consider only the most promising and direct challenge to my claim that any moral system capable of prescribing the destruction of some moral agents is self-defeating. A moral system might explicitly limit its obligation to destroy moral agents with a superordinate principle proscribing the annihilation of all moral agents. Such a system could not be dismissed simply because of the bizarre actuarial calculations to which it would commit us. Furthermore, since our obligations commonly depend on others' past or anticipated actions, the coordination this system demands does not suffice to reject it. If this type of moral system is unacceptable, it must be due to some problem arising from the interaction between the system's destructive principles and its curb upon them.

Before proceeding, the requirement that moral systems not be self-defeating must be distinguished from a principle placing a ceiling on the destruction of moral agents. The criterion of adequacy states that it cannot be obligatory to halt moral interaction, whereas the destruction-limiting principle states that it is obligatory not to halt moral interaction. The criterion of adequacy, unlike the disaster-avoidance principle, is compatible with the proposition that halting moral interaction can be permissible. If a destructive ceiling is to guarantee that destructive obligations will not proliferate to such an extent that the moral system prescribing them will prove self-defeating, it must take precedence over obligations to destroy moral agents whenever it is germane. In short, a moral system that avoids self-defeatism by prohibiting the avoidable cessation of moral intercourse must posit an absolute duty not to halt moral interaction.

It is doubtful, however, that anyone would want to accept all of the consequences of this incontrovertible principle. Consider a moral system that prescribes executing murderers but prohibits stopping moral interaction. Its possible application to a grotesquely degenerate society in which every adult has committed murder and a single innocent child survives exposes its alarming implications. Suppose that circumstances evolve in such a way that one of these adults must choose between executing the legions of murderers, herself included, and torturing this blameless child slowly to death. Not only is it probable that this villainous individual's propensities would incline her to opt for torturing the child, but also her moral code would recommend, indeed it would exact, this choice from her. But surely, in this predicament, preferring the demise of a thoroughly corrupt moral community to a desperate teleology of self-perpetuation would be a defensible stance. If so, the moral system's destructive ceiling cannot be absolute. But if this moral system prescribes executions without categorically ruling out prescribed annihilation, it is self-defeating.

The preceding argument might elicit diametric responses—outrage or indifference. On the assumption that any situations in which the requirement that moral systems not be self-defeating would come into conflict with a principle dictating the perpetuation of moral interaction are very unlikely to occur, this argument might be dismissed as practically vacuous musing. But contrariwise, once it is realized that a moral system which is not self-defeating would be obliged to affirm the permissibility of both alternatives, this argument might be condemned for its failure to take a firm stand against torturing the child. If the ban on self-defeatism in moral systems does not seem irrelevant, it may seem morally bankrupt.

The negative criterion of adequacy I have advocated implies a plurality of ultimate principles which dominate other principles but which themselves may not always be reconcilable. To deny that an adequate moral system can be self-defeating is to grant that the survival of a moral community is a supreme value (that is why moral systems cannot prescribe the extinction of moral relations) but that the avoidance of degradation is, too (that is why moral systems cannot prescribe savage measures to avert the dissolution of moral relations). Underlying this view of the structure of moral systems is the assumption that moral tragedy is possible because human acumen does not extend to definitively balancing and ordering all values and disvalues. Though some persons reflecting on the dilemma sketched above may be appalled at the conclusion that no adequate moral system could prescribe the executions rather than the torture session, it is not obvious that a bloodbath ending in silence or, perhaps, in a lone child's crying is morally superior to a single monstrous act. Sometimes persons are forced to choose between ultimate values, but no consensus about these formidable quandaries has even endured. The fundamental reason for rejecting self-defeating moral systems, then, is that they refuse to recognize limits on competent moral judgment and therefore fail to demarcate the bounds of moral responsibility.

Still, someone might admit that the question of whether moral systems can introduce principles to block destructive obligations when they threaten the future of moral interaction is telling for a theory of *in extremis* ethics and yet contend that this problem can safely be ignored by moral systems designed to cope with a normal range of cases. While it is undeniable that only farfetched situations can bring destructive obligations into conflict with destructive ceilings, the requirement that moral systems not be self-defeating has critical normative consequences in more familiar contexts. Specifically, no moral system that satisfies this criterion can require its adherents to destroy moral agents. Since ordinary morality must address life and death issues, the question which has been posed in an *in extremis* setting cannot finally be eluded.

It is important to appreciate that reasons drawn from remote predicaments do not provide the only support for excluding obligations to destroy moral agents from adequate moral systems. This constraint on moral prescription is borne out to a surprising degree by everyday beliefs and practices. We think, for instance, that killing in self-defense and euthanasia are permissible, not compulsory. Moreover, although it is tempting to think that soldiers engaged in justifiable combat are obligated to kill enemy troops, it is not killing but incapacitating the enemy that is clearly required in order to win the war. Capturing enemy prisoners is not an abdication of duty. Also, if there were a weapon that harmlessly paralyzed enemy soldiers long enough to disarm them, we would think it wrong to use guns and bombs instead. Still, we might be inclined to say killing is mandatory in the case of a fiend like Hitler, yet it is by no means self-evident that the evil individual deserves the release of death nor that high-minded causes are best served by brutal means. Looking at the problem from a different angle, our reluctance to inure children to killing also confirms that we are not convinced that we have obligations to destroy moral agents. If we had convictions to the contrary, it would be unconscionable not to prepare children to do their duty. Yet, we evidently prefer to instill in them a presumption against killing that is so stringent that it would be unfair to blame anyone for refusing to kill.

Plainly, we do not condemn every instance of killing, but moral intuition does not conclusively ratify the proposition that we are morally obligated to kill. Although it would fly in the face of common knowledge to maintain that no one regards any form of killing as obligatory, some of our abiding beliefs and practices constitute notable exceptions to the assumption that killing must be either right or wrong.[9] Acceptance of self-defeatism as a negative criterion of adequacy for moral systems captures the gist of these beliefs and practices and integrates this viewpoint into the structure of moral systems; rejection of this criterion leaves these beliefs and practices anomalous.

6. Admissible Permissions

Someone might now observe that situations do arise in which losses of moral agents are unavoidable, and the only question is which losses will be incurred. Confronted with this sort of dilemma, a moral system must acknowledge that some sacrifice is permissible though it cannot, for the reasons developed above, obligate anyone to sacrifice himself or to dispatch another. Necessary though it is, this concession is troubling because introducing permissions to cope with such situations may seem to spirit in destructive obligations as well. If it should prove to be permissible to execute a particular criminal, the obligation to treat similar cases similarly might take over and might automatically generate an obligation to impose this sentence in every relevantly similar case that subsequently arises. Thus, destructive obligations appear to follow from destructive permissions.

This problem cannot be handled by claiming that destructive permissions are self-limiting inasmuch as they are only granted in exceptional circumstances. It is not impossible that the extraordinary will become commonplace. Furthermore, the claim that destructive permissions are only countenanced in unique predicaments is tinged with sophistry. Appeals to hair-splitting, morally questionable distinctions or to chancy predictions about the course of future events cannot decisively circumvent the difficulty at hand.

Instead, it is necessary to examine the proposition that permissions in combination with the obligation to treat similar cases similarly generate new obligations. Consider an archetypal obligation like the obligation to tell the truth. Could this moral requirement be understood as a product of the conjunction of permissible honest practices and the obligation to treat similar cases similarly? Surely not. We are obligated to conduct ourselves honestly, not because we are permitted to do so and consistency obliges us to routinize our practice, but because deceit (for reasons too complicated to go into here) is bad.[10] Clear instances of obligation are supported by reasons independent of and stronger than the desirability of consistency.

Now, let us compare the moral force of an obligation with that of a paradigmatic permission in virtue of a compelling moral reason, such as the permission to decline an unwanted invitation by falsely pleading a prior engagement. Though it is permissible and usual for recipients of burdensome invitations to spare their importuning hosts' feelings by lying, it is not obligatory to conform to this practice. A person who sometimes refuses invitations with tactful honesty and sometimes resorts to white lies does nothing wrong. Permissible practices, regardless of how entrenched they may become, are not automatically metamorphosed into obligations through the intervention of the obligation to treat similar cases similarly. Indeed, there would be no permissions if permissions were nullified as soon as they were exercised.

Since the permission to use deceptive stratagems to avoid unwanted social commitments is a trivial one, it might yet be urged that important permissions which allow the destruction of moral agents ought to be wielded uniformly. But it is not clear that the obligation to treat similar cases similarly is any more restrictive in regard to important permissions than it is in regard to trivial ones. For example, killing in self-defense is permissible and can involve destroying moral agents. Nevertheless, a person who responds violently to assault on one occasion and submits quiescently to a similar attack on another occasion cannot be morally castigated for inconsistency. The claim that permission to destroy moral agents must be exercised consistently is only plausible when the permission is conferred on the state. In permissibly executing one individual, the state seems to promulgate a policy which it is not free to implement erratically. Perhaps, then, the obligation to treat similar cases similarly can convert state, but not private, permissions to destroy moral agents into obligations to do so.

While the citizen's need for predictable public policy provides a powerful reason supporting consistency in this arena, it does not transform state permissions into state obligations. What it does is to establish a presumption favoring continuance of existing permissible practices but not precluding modifications or reversals. If the state is to be rigidly committed to unfailing regularity once it has exercised a permission bearing on moral agency, it will need compelling reasons at the outset for opting to exercise its permission one way rather than

Contribution of Inalienable Rights 51

another. These reasons will pluck the policy from the realm of permissibility and lodge it in the realm of obligation. But, in that case, it is not the stricture of consistency but the reasons for adopting the policy that generate the obligation.

I have argued that neither the state nor anyone else can have obligations to destroy moral agents. It follows either that destroying moral agents is never permissible or that permissions to destroy moral agents are never transformed into destructive obligations. Since destruction of at least one moral agent is sometimes inevitable, it is clear that this form of destruction can be permissible and, therefore, that these permissions do not conceal destructive obligations.

7. Inalienable Rights

When circumstances call for sacrifices that moral systems cannot impose and a person elects to sacrifice himself for the benefit of others, he undertakes action that is of necessity supererogatory. While the moral system cannot prescribe the sacrifice, it must permit it and applaud its altruistic intent. Those altruistic sacrifices that would render a moral system self-defeating if it were ever to declare them obligatory are supererogatory whenever they are done in appropriate circumstances. Inalienable rights are the moral instruments through which moral systems implement both these restraints on moral prescription and these critical permissions.

Conscientious renunciation of a right entails a prima facie obligation to refrain from interfering with the uses others may make of the object of the right. If it is impossible to be obligated to let others do what they want with the objects of some rights, it is impossible to renounce these rights conscientiously. I have argued that moral systems cannot prescribe the destruction of moral agents. A consequence of this limitation is that moral systems cannot require moral agents to relinquish goods which are necessary for moral agency. Though a satisfactory moral system can condone altruistic sacrifice of these goods as supererogatory in some circumstances, it cannot countenance obligations to sacrifice the same goods.[11] Since moral systems must exclude obligations to sacrifice goods needed for moral agency, any rights entitling persons to these goods must bar conscientious renunciation.

Two complementary necessary conditions for inalienable rights are implicit in my account of conscientious renunciation:

1. An inalienable right has an object that it is never obligatory, though it may be supererogatory, to sacrifice altruistically.
2. An inalienable right protects a good that individuals require in order to function as moral agents, that is, to choose and to adhere to a code of conduct sensitive to the interests of others.

These criteria suggest corresponding methods for identifying candidates for inalienability. The first is the more intuitive. Proposed rights can be appraised from the standpoint of our convictions about situations in which an individual could properly sacrifice the object of the right. The question is whether there is any situation in which we are compelled to admit that the sacrifice would be obligatory. If there are no circumstances in which anyone could be obligated to tolerate treatment that would abridge the right, the right may well be inalienable. The second criterion allows for greater rigor and can serve as a check on overly harsh or lenient intuitions about morality in exceptional circumstances. This test involves determining whether or not the right sustains moral agency by contributing to a core of security that persons need in order to conduct themselves morally. Together these procedures provide a way to find out whether a moral system must rule out conscientious renunciation of a right in order not to be self-defeating. Any right that survives this test is a strong contender for inclusion in the class of inalienable rights. If it also proves to be immune to renunciation by fiat, it must be inalienable.[12]

3

Four Inalienable Rights

Securing moral agency is a fundamental desideratum of moral systems which is achieved through the offices of inalienable rights. A moral system would fail in this critical objective if it could require rightholders to relinquish the goods to which inalienable rights entitle them or could prescribe abridgments of inalienable rights. To give substance to this position, it is now necessary to defend a list of candidate rights by appraising them against the two criteria obtained in the preceding chapter. I shall urge that the following rights satisfy those criteria:

1. the right to life, i.e., the right not to be killed
2. the right to personal liberty, i.e., the right not to be forced to execute another person's dictates
3. the right to benign treatment, i.e., the right not to suffer gratuitous acute pain
4. the right to satisfaction of basic needs, i.e., the right to adequate food, water, clothing, shelter, and medical treatment for survival

Each of these rights has an object which it is supererogatory whenever appropriate to sacrifice altruistically and which is necessary for persons to exercise moral agency. Consequently, none of them can be renounced conscientiously.

1. The Right to Life and the Right to Personal Liberty

The right to life prohibits other persons from killing the person who possesses the right and allows this person to defend himself if he is attacked. It is obvious that a person cannot be a moral agent unless he is alive (at least, not within the moral sphere in which we presently find ourselves), and so it is also obvious that this right protects something essential to moral agency. But it is doubtful that it is always supererogatory when it is appropriate for a person to sacrifice his life for the benefit of others. Two representative cases can be adduced to call this claim into question: 1) a soldier has a duty to follow orders to participate in battles if her army is involved in a just war, and 2) a citizen may have a duty to join her country's army in wartime.

These proposed counterexamples can be dispensed with quite easily. A soldier is obligated to fight in battles or to care for wounded combatants in the midst of battles because she has agreed to do so in voluntarily signing up. Without this contract, there is no obligation to participate in a war for the benefit of persons other than the soldier. As for civilians who are obligated to volunteer for military service in a time of war, they are only obligated to join the army and to risk their lives if the war is defensive. In other words, it is only when a person would be fighting to protect her own interests as well as others' that she is duty-bound to join her country's army. A person is not obligated to help further a ruler's aggressive designs, nor is a person governed by a tyrant obligated to help resist liberating forces. Evidently, persons are not obligated to endanger their lives for altruistic reasons unless they have entered into agreements that commit them to conduct that would otherwise be supererogatory.[1]

Still, it is important to emphasize that there is a morally significant difference between a right-holder's risking his life and his sacrificing his life. On the one hand, a soldier can enter a battle with the understanding that there is a considerable risk of her being killed but without any intention of sacrificing her life. On the other hand, a soldier can pounce on a live hand grenade in order to absorb the explosion and save the nearby members of her platoon with the understanding that there is no chance of her surviving. Somewhere between these cases the distinction between a risk and a sacrifice blurs, for it is not possible to say precisely how grave a risk must be before it becomes a sacrifice, and it is not always possible to find out how grave a risk is. Nevertheless, this distinction is sufficiently firm to be useful. Conscientious military commanders acknowledge it by asking for volunteers when a mission thought to be suicidal is planned. Because prior agreements cannot obligate persons to sacrifice their lives though they can obligate them to risk this loss, it would be wrong for an officer to presume to sacrifice the lives of her soliders on the strength of their induction into the army. Regardless of past commitments, a person's altruistic sacrifice of her life remains supererogatory.

The right to personal liberty protects right-holders from being forced to execute another person's dictates. This right, too, bears on moral agency straightforwardly since we do not hold persons responsible for their behavior when they have been compelled to act by others. Still, it is somewhat difficult to see how the concept of supererogation pertains to this right. Clearly, a person may be obligated to act on another's behalf and exclusively for the other's benefit. But the right to personal liberty does not entitle persons never to do anyone else's bidding; rather it entitles persons not to be *forced* to carry out another person's order. Consequently, supererogation involving a sacrifice of the object of this right must consist of submitting to coercion for someone else's benefit.

An example will bring out the difference between sacrificing personal liberty and acting as another person's agent. Suppose that a war is in progress. Two scientists in collaboration have nearly completed plans for a new weapon that is expected to overpower the enemy quickly and humanely. Enemy agents kidnap one of the scientists in order to extract the plans for the weapon from her. The other scientist knows that her colleague will be threatened with torture, will almost certainly give in, and will probably flay herself with reproaches for the rest of her life. To save her from this misery, the other scientist arranges for her colleague's release by agreeing to take her place. Naturally, she realizes that her captors will try to force her to divulge the weapon plans and that she may comply, but she is determined to spare her associate. In substituting herself for her colleague, the samaritan plainly advances this other individual's interests but assumes no responsibility to behave as her beneficiary would wish her to; she submits to subjugation in order that her friend be freed but not in order to represent her.

What is involved in relinquishing personal liberty is twofold: subjection to a formidable threat of harm coupled with anticipation of heteronomous compliance shattering to the agent's integrity. Whether a person can be obligated to endure acute pain or severe deprivation for someone else's benefit, that is, whether a person can be obligated to withstand coercive threats, will be addressed with respect to the rights to benign treatment and satisfaction of basic needs. At this point, it suffices to note that acquiescing to certain kinds of force betrays the self and leaves the victim confused about his beliefs and affectionate bonds as well as contemptuous of himself. It is hard to see how anyone could be obligated to sacrifice the unity of his personality in this way since such dissociation impairs and may destroy the individual's ability to live a rewarding life.

2. Force, Liberties, and Law

The right to personal liberty raises numerous problems.[2] One is that the concept of force seems to be relative to the individual to whom force is being applied. Since what will force one person to do a given act may not force someone else to do the same act, what will count as respect for the right to personal liberty apparently varies with the strength of will of the person who possesses the right. However, this variability is not peculiar to the right to personal liberty. Whether an action is a violation of someone's right to life depends on the victim's susceptibility, too. It is hard, for example, to gun down a person wearing a bulletproof vest, but it is easy to kill a hemophiliac. And for similar reasons, some persons may resist coercive measures to which others would readily acquiesce. Nevertheless, it is a mistake to infer that these differences prevent persons from respecting rights to life and personal liberty.

Without denying that human vulnerability varies and that an action that may violate one person's right to life may inflict no serious harm on another (compare scratching a hemophiliac with scratching most people), we regard a standardized range of actions as attempted violations of this right. If an agent has been informed of another person's unusual vulnerability, he can be condemned for neglecting it or for taking advantage of it; also, if an agent ought to inquire about unusual vulnerabilities—as physicians are obligated to ask patients about drug allergies before prescribing medication—he can be condemned for acting in ignorance. Yet, for quotidian purposes persons are sufficiently similar with respect to their inveterate weaknesses, and their abnormal weaknesses are often sufficiently noticeable that it is reasonable to confine the core conception of an attempted violation of the right to life to the actions these familiar conditions prohibit.

In a parallel fashion, attempted violations of the right to personal liberty involve a command accompanied by a threat of harm or by a sample infliction of harm of a degree of fearfulness such that we would expect an ordinary person to submit and his refraining from submitting, if he does refuse to comply, requires that he marshall greater volitional stamina than most people have at their disposal. (I leave aside nonviolent coercion employing biochemical or psychic means since these are as yet largely the province of science fiction and would not alter the present argument.) No form of persuasion that does not include a threat or a preliminary injury can count as a violation of the right to personal liberty. Although uncommon impressionability exposes a person to more violations of his right to personal liberty than a less easily influenced person may suffer, while uncommon fortitude immunizes a person to some violations of this right, the class of attempted violations for which persons can ordinarily be blamed is demarcated by the extent of typical endurance limits.

The right to personal liberty specifies a range of harms that others may not inflict on the bearer of the right in order to obtain his submission. But this right mentions nothing that a right-holder is free to do. Basic liberties of the type enumerated by John Rawls are, perhaps, conspicuously absent from my list of inalienable rights.[3]

I have barred forced obedience without affirming any areas of discretion because the right to personal liberty does, but basic liberties do not, meet the criteria for inalienable rights. Depending on a person's circumstances and inclinations, it would not necessarily be supererogatory for her to give up the opportunity to run for political office or to publish her ideas; however, she could never be obligated to expose herself to forced compliance with another person's wishes. Moreover, the right to personal liberty has an immediate impact on moral agency, whereas basic liberties are only derivatively pertinent to moral agency. What liberties a person ought to have concerns the purview of moral agency as opposed to moral agency itself.

A person's freedom to express herself or to act can be circumscribed, and yet she may remain a moral agent. In fact, unjust restrictions can be imposed on her liberty without neutralizing her ability to function as a moral agent. A person who is not allowed under any circumstances to make any statement criticizing the government of her country is subject to an unjust limitation of her personal liberty, but her pronouncements do not therefore cease to have any moral stature. Still, someone might object that the same results can be laboriously achieved through detailed and thoroughgoing restrictions on liberty as can be achieved through coercive orders.

An unusually tenacious and patient censor might disallow every statement a person proposes to make by a process of elimination until only one conceivable statement on the subject at hand was left. The objection is that this progressive narrowing of the prospective speaker's options would have the same effect as the ruler's simply telling the speaker what she must say to avert punishment. But this claim will not survive close scrutiny. The censor's restrictions on what the speaker may say always leave the speaker the option of remaining silent without incurring any penalty; however, a tyrant's ordering the speaker to make a particular assertion and threatening to harm her if she refuses closes off all alternatives. Thus, restrictions on personal liberty, regardless of how rigidly they confine a person's range of options, never become equivalent to coerced action.

Only an enforced denial of personal liberty can usurp moral agency because an enforced denial of personal liberty is indistinguishable from coerced inaction. A person whose liberty to speak is effectively denied is not permitted to assert anything just as a person who is intimidated into silence is prevented from saying anything. If a person were denied all freedom to act, she would be immobilized unless further violations of her right not to be forced to execute another person's dictates enlivened her in the guise of someone else's puppet. From this, it is clear that some freedom to act is necessary for moral agency though no single liberty or combination of liberties can be identified as necessary for moral agency.

By ruling out both coerced inaction and coerced action, the right to personal liberty rules out a total denial of freedom to act yet stops short of fixing the boundaries of personal liberty. The question of the rightful scope of individual autonomy, that is, what liberties political institutions should guarantee and which decisions legislation should not intervene in, falls within the province of a theory of justice. A theory of inalienable rights can make only a negative contribution to these issues, namely, that personal liberty must be constrained by the inalienable rights of others. Beyond this, a theory of inalienable rights is not competent to venture unless it can be shown that one and only one set of choices must be left to persons who could not forgo them except supererogatorily and whose status as moral agents would be imperiled without them.

Since there seems to be no basis for delimiting such a set, these matters are best referred to a theory of justice. Thus, the right to personal liberty disallows paralyzing agency through imposed conduct but recognizes that the range of options legally available to agents may be restricted justifiably.

At this point, it might be urged that the right to personal liberty commits us to utopian anarchism because it rules out legal, as opposed to voluntary, restriction of liberty. The right to personal liberty seems to be incompatible with any law that prohibits a specified type of conduct, such as murder, or requires a specified type of conduct, such as paying income tax, and enforces its dictates through sanctions. Is it, then, possible to curb freedom to act using the law as a tool of enforcement without violating the right to personal liberty?

Consider the plight of a person who is contemplating murder. Supposing that it would be best for her to refrain from doing this, we must ask how the law might enter into her deliberations. There are three possibilities: 1) she realizes that murder would be wrong regardless of what the law says and decides against it; 2) she wants to commit murder, but the law deters her; and 3) she decides to commit murder and defies the law. The law's influence in a person's life differs in two respects from the influence of a robber's pointed pistol over a bank teller's conduct or the influence of a kidnapper's ransom demands over a parent's course of action. First, the law and its penalties may not occur as a factor in a person's deliberations despite the fact that she is contemplating an illegal act and is familiar with the law since she may conclude on independent grounds that the act would be undesirable, if not wrong. Second, in deciding to defy the law she is taking a gamble that she will not be caught and punished. For the bank teller or the parent of an abducted child, the threat is immediate and inescapable, and the probability of incurring injury for failing to comply with the robber's or kidnapper's demands must be assumed to be certain.

Though law cannot be adequately analyzed in terms of commands backed by threats, a law that prohibits an action that a person is considering doing certainly can assume that visage.[4] However, the command and the threat are both more remote from the person to whom these are addressed than is ordinarily the case when commands are issued and threats are hurled. Indeed, it would be misleading to say that a person who never seriously contemplates committing murder is submitting to a legal order not to kill anyone in order to avoid being punished. It is only when a person actually considers violating the law that he may encounter the threatening aspect of the law. Accordingly, it is better to think of certain laws as permanent, or at least stable, possibilities of threats rather than as blades constantly poised above every citizen's neck. An individual must engage the law by proposing to commit a crime in order for the law's deterrent function to be activated.

The above view of legal deterrence helps to reconcile the rule of law with the right to personal liberty. A law does not force a person to act in one way rather than another unless he takes steps to violate it, and even then the law may not intervene. Admittedly, when statutes are unacceptably invasive and occasionally when persons initiate unacceptable projects, the law abridges the right to personal liberty. Still, properly understood, the problem of the relation between law and liberty does not concern the compatibility of law and the right to personal liberty but rather the justifiability of given legal sanctions. Obviously, it is possible for laws to be enacted that violate the right to personal liberty. Laws forbidding harmless sexual practices between consenting adults fall within this category. Nevertheless, the gravity of some crimes is sufficient to justify deterrent measures. Where this is the case, the law is capable of abridging a person's right to personal liberty but would do so permissibly.[5]

The right to personal liberty, as Locke knew, protects right-holders from the arbitrary interference of other persons. It does not license right-holders to do anything they please, and it does not bar officials from enforcing legitimate limits on action. Scrupulous officials exact conformity from right-holders primarily in the name of justice and sometimes for the sake of tolerable order in social life, whereas the right to personal liberty exempts right-holders only from coerced compliance with the private dictates of other individuals. Thus, even when a person is sorely tempted to commit a crime and refrains solely for fear of punishment, his right to personal liberty is not violated unless the law is unwarranted.

3. The Right to Benign Treatment and the Right to Satisfaction of Basic Needs

The right to benign treatment and the right to satisfaction of basic needs are a step removed from moral agency as compared with the right to life and the right to personal liberty. A successful violation of a person's right to life destroys the person and along with him his ability to function as a moral agent. A successful violation of a person's right to personal liberty constitutes a temporary or permanent usurpation of his moral agency. In contrast to this, violations of the right to benign treatment or the right to satisfaction of basic needs can be used as a means of destroying or usurping moral agency. By subjecting a person to acute pain or depriving him of basic necessities, another person can kill or control him. Thus, one reason for listing these rights as inalienable rights is their instrumental relation to the two I have already established.[6] But not all violations of the rights to benign treatment and satisfaction of basic needs impinge on the victim's right to life or personal liberty. A person could be subjected to terrible pain that is not life-threatening or could be kept desperately needy but alive, and this maltreatment could be inflicted unaccompanied by any order to which the victim could acquiesce and gain reprieve. Since the rights to benign treatment and satisfaction of basic needs provide a form of protection for moral agency that is independent of survival and personal liberty, it is necessary to accord them full status as separate inalienable rights.

The right to benign treatment is equivalent to the right not to suffer acute gratuitous pain. Although it is ordinarily wrong to inflict mild pain on a person gratuitously, this proscription does not derive from any inalienable right since mild pain does not undermine moral agency. A person's possession of the right to benign treatment forbids torturing him or assaulting him, but it also forbids withholding analgesics when acute pain can be relieved or a cure for the cause of the pain when one is available. Persons are entitled to these forms of consideration because acute pain sabotages moral agency. That we think this is so is confirmed both by our not requiring an agonized individual to take others' interests into account to the usual degree and by our willingness to justify or forgive otherwise reprehensible schemes that an acutely pained individual might undertake in order to obtain surcease. Insofar as acute pain is unavoidable and unredeemed by anticipation of a good outcome, moral relations are fragile, but insofar as human suffering can be alleviated moral relations can be preserved.

The right to satisfaction of basic needs provides for adequate food, water, clothing, shelter, and medical treatment for survival and thereby protects right-holders from certain types of deprivation.[7] The right to satisfaction of basic needs is an umbrella right covering an assortment of subsidiary rights, but it should be stressed that the subsidiary rights meet three criteria. First, the rights prevent forms of deprivation that cause acute pain or ultimately the death of the victim; basic needs are critical. Second, they secure things that all people need occasionally though the intervals at which the need arises may not be regular; basic needs are universal. Third, the objects of the rights are goods that people ordinarily provide for themselves but sometimes cannot; basic needs are personal. In sum, basic needs are usually satisfied, and unsatisfied basic needs leave any individual *in extremis*.

Since severe deprivation often causes acute pain, it might be tempting to treat the right to satisfaction of basic needs merely as a means of respecting the right to benign treatment. However, this relegation would overlook the complexities of the relation between the right to satisfaction of basic needs and moral agency. While it is undeniable that one reason for acknowledging the right to satisfaction of basic needs is that withholding the goods secured by this right may cause acute pain and thus impair moral agency, this is not the only way that violations of this right can disable moral agents. Prolonged malnutrition or chronic disease may cause relatively mild discomfort but induce obsessive preoccupation with self-preservation or insurmountable lassitude. These latter conditions may prevent the victim from recognizing and fulfilling his obligations. Furthermore, whether deprivation is extremely painful or not, unrelieved incremental deprivation eventually kills the sufferer and thereby destroys moral agency just as violations of the right to life do. Because the right to satisfaction of basic needs sustains moral agency in three distinct ways and ministers to human frailty by providing for goods that no other right guarantees, it is an independent right that complements but is not subordinate to the right to benign treatment.

The right to satisfaction of basic needs is sometimes rejected on the grounds that it promises the impossible. There may not be enough of some essential commodity or service to go around. Furthermore, respect for the right depends on agricultural, technological, and medical expertise, and these applied sciences have advanced slowly. Since this is so, the right to satisfaction of basic needs seems to entitle persons to nothing at all or, at any rate, nothing definite. But the right to satisfaction of basic needs does not differ from the rights of the classic liberal tradition in this regard. Variations in supplies of needed goods and in the sophistication of knowledge over the course of history have affected respect for the rights to life and personal liberty, too.

Insufficient personnel and outmoded equipment sometimes diminish enforcement of the rights to life and personal liberty. Moreover, ignorance can result in unavoidable abridgments of these rights. For instance, there might be key words which persons could say to gain control over others and thereby abridge their rights to personal liberty. If 'abracadabra' were such a word but nobody knew it, a person joking with a friend could utter what she believed to be the nonsense syllables 'abracadabra' and then, in proposing that her friend go jump in the lake, innocently force her unsuspecting companion to comply with her suggestion. An individual's right to personal liberty would have been abridged, but the perpetrator would not realize that she had committed any wrong and would not know how she could have avoided committing it. More realistically, doctors have not always understood which of their regimens would prove fatal to their patients. Uncontrollable circumstances can limit our ability to respect any right. Gradual progress in science does not demonstrate that there are no rights; rather, it improves our ability to respect all rights, including the right to satisfaction of basic needs.[8]

4. Supererogatory Pain and Deprivation

Many of the most widely known examples of supererogation involve acute pain. To submit to torture so that someone else will not be tortured, to make oneself the target of an attack in order to deflect it from someone else, to give someone else pain killers when one desperately needs them oneself, or to allow someone else to be cured of a painful disease rather than oneself are all supererogatory acts. The only plausible objection to the claim that benign treatment cannot be sacrificed obligatorily relies on the case of a parent attracting an assailant to herself in order to protect her young child.

In situations in which this or similar conduct might seem to be obligatory, two features stand out. First, by virtue of the parent-child relationship the parent has a more stringent and a more extensive obligation to aid the child than people ordinarily have with respect to one another. Conduct that does not count as supererogatory when parents act in relation to their young children, like allowing their children to live in their homes, would count as supererogatory if a person acted in a similar way on behalf of total strangers under ordinary circumstances. Second, whereas the child is helpless, the parent has some ability to defend herself and to understand her pain. Consequently, this adult may incur less serious injury and may suffer less from whatever injury is inflicted. Thus, the parent's intervention represents an attempt to minimize the harm caused by the attacker.

In a situation in which a parent is forced to choose between submitting to excruciating pain and allowing her child to be subjected to the same treatment and there is no possibility of resistance, we would hesitate to say that a parent's agreeing to endure the pain instead of her child would not be supererogatory.[9] A parent's self-sacrificial conduct is unquestionably more comprehensible than that of a complete stranger would be since the parent's love for her child helps to explain her ability to act selflessly. Nevertheless, neither the comparative ease with which we can understand parental self-sacrifice nor uncritical acceptance of conventional expectations about maternal self-sacrifice should seduce us into dismissing such conduct as mere obligation fulfillment. A special relationship can generate an obligation to endure greater pain for the sake of another person than would ordinarily be required and to take greater risks of suffering pain than would ordinarily be required; however, the obligation is limited by the degree and certainty of the torment.

It is more difficult to exhibit the supererogatory quality of action pertaining to the right to satisfaction of basic needs. To some extent, this is because of the complexity of the system through which our basic needs are satisfied. We do not periodically line up to receive minimally adequate allotments of food, water, medical treatment, clothing, and shelter; monetary and property systems are interposed between individuals and the things they need. Consequently, it is difficult to pinpoint which transfers of money or property constitute indirect sacrifices of basic necessities. Moreover, many of us live so far above subsistence level that it is difficult to conceive what it would be like to be on the brink of starvation for lack of nourishment, dehydration for lack of water, expiring for lack of medical treatment, or freezing for lack of clothing or shelter. Still, it is possible to enhance empathic powers by artificially simplifying matters.

Imagine a society consisting of ten people living in isolation on almost barren land. Because their land is barely arable and they have no alternative source of supplies, they live on the verge of starvation. Each day they search for food and then gather to prepare and eat a single poor meal. They take turns serving the meal and always line up in the same order with the person at the head of the line rotating. Sometimes there is not enough food for everyone to receive a minimally adequate portion. When this happens, the members of the group have agreed that minimally adequate portions should be dispensed to as many people in the line as can be served before the food runs out. They hold that it is better for some of them to eat enough than for all of them to eat too little because experience has shown that the ones who have eaten adequately will be more successful in finding food the next day than all ten of them would be in an undernourished condition. One day the ninth person in line receives the last helping of food leaving nothing for the server. Can the ninth person be obligated to relinquish her meal to the tenth or to share it with her? Surely not. Though persons may have an obligation to share a surplus with others who are desperate, there does not seem to be any basis for arguing that persons are obligated to give up commodities or services without which they themselves will eventually perish.

Despite the practical difficulties that could arise in connection with distinguishing intense hunger from malnutrition, severe thirst from dehydration, extreme vulnerability from exposure or medical neglect, and postponed gratification from sacrifice, it seems to be clear that people cannot be obligated to subject themselves to starvation, dehydration, exposure, or malady for the sake of their fellows. These conditions inflict such misery on people and bring them so close to death that the moral strictures associated with the rights to life and benign treatment carry over to the right to satisfaction of basic needs. A person must enjoy an excess of an essential commodity before he can be obligated to distribute any of his allotment to others; lacking such an excess, his forgoing any part of his portion for the benefit of others would be supererogatory.

5. A Note on Property Rights

At this point, someone might interject that a person who has obtained a surplus of essential commodities cannot be obligated (though he may be inclined) to help sustain others who have less than they need. Charity, on this view, cannot be obligatory because this obligation would conflict with property rights, and property rights, it might be argued, are necessary to secure satisfaction of basic needs.[10] My present concerns do not require that all forms of obligatory benevolence be systematically delineated, but it is necessary to consider whether the right to satisfaction of basic needs masks powerful property rights.

One way to formulate this problem is to ask whether the nine members of my impoverished hypothetical society who receive food on a day when there is not enough for ten are in the same position with respect to their portions as we are with respect to a particular meal in which we have a property right. At the outset, the nine people who have been served portions do seem to have rudimentary property rights in the food they have received. Each member of the group, including the person who receives no food, is expected to allow the others to consume the food they have been given.[11] The daily distribution of rations sets up a system of possessions backed by conventions of mutual restraint. Still, the persons who receive food are only free to use it for the purpose for which it was intended. Each has a right to satisfaction of her need for nourishment. Therefore each is entitled to eat the food she is given, but none is entitled to waste her portion or to feed it to a pet. Of course, property rights are usually limited. A person who has a property right in a particular meal may not use the meal to kill someone by adding poison to it and serving it to a chosen victim. Nevertheless, property rights do not usually impose an obligation to use the property in only one prescribed way. Although a person cannot use a meal to murder or injure someone else, the owner is not required to use it for nourishment. In contradistinction to this, the rights of the nine members of my straitened society are contingent upon their using their food to satisfy a basic need.

The right to satisfaction of basic needs could develop into a property right. If my society of ten were to allow its members to use their portions as they please within the constraints imposed by the rights of others, they would create a conditional property right. The portion each person received would become her property provided that there was enough for everyone. However, this society could, instead, require that anyone who did not want to eat her share return it to the communal pot from which it would be dispensed to the others in order to improve their diet a bit. This alternative suggests a way of differentiating the right to satisfaction of basic needs from property rights.

The right to satisfaction of basic needs does not predetermine how issues concerning the distribution of essential commodities should be settled once a society meets the basic needs of its members. If the recipients of excess essential commodities forfeit their allotments upon putting them to some innovative use, they cannot be said to have a property right in these commodities. Alternatively, if they are allowed to use an allotment that exceeds their requirements for some unrelated purpose, their right to satisfaction of basic needs is transformed into a property right. Nevertheless, neither of these arrangements is a logical consequence of the right to satisfaction of basic needs. Because this right confers commodities and services on persons and prohibits interference with their use of these allotments, it is reasonable to construe the right to satisfaction of basic needs as a precursor of property rights. But because the protection afforded by this right terminates after each individual's basic needs have been met, it is not defensible to claim that the right to satisfaction of basic needs is really a camouflaged property right.

A slightly different way to understand the relation between the right to satisfaction of basic needs and property rights is to reflect on how the former could be implemented. In order to ensure clarity, I have confined my discussion to the simplest conceivable method of guaranteeing this right—persons line up and receive provisions that they have gathered earlier that day. But this arrangement is neither practicable nor desirable in modern societies. Manufacturing and farming on a gigantic scale have replaced the daily subsistence harvest of my imaginary society, and complex systems of private and state ownership, taxation, and transfer payments have replaced my simple communal dole. Although detailed proposals for implementing the right to satisfaction of basic needs are beyond the scope of this inquiry, it is worth noting some basic points in regard to this matter.

The choice between private and collective ownership of the means of production is not settled by advocacy of the right to satisfaction of basic needs. Since both capitalism and socialism are in principle capable of generating sufficient wealth to implement the right to satisfaction of basic needs, this right does not dictate a decision between alternate economic systems except if conditions are such that under one, but not the other, system this right could not be secured for all who qualify. Nevertheless, it is incontrovertible that a system of personal property involving both money and goods provides the most efficient mechanism for supplying individuals with what they need to survive since this arrangement frees them from dependence on remote channels and allows them to choose the goods best suited to their needs. Furthermore, introducing a monetary system to mediate between state officials, individual recipients, and essential commodities reduces an official's ability to use her dispensations to violate a recipient's right to personal liberty. Although the institution of personal property is

Four Inalienable Rights

not a necessary consequence of the right to satisfaction of basic needs, it is only in exceptionally dire or primitive circumstances that other arrangements appear attractive or viable.

6. Supererogation and Promising

The most convincing rejoinders to the connection I have drawn between supererogation and sacrifice of life, personal liberty, benign treatment, and basic necessities capitalize on a pair of insights. First, persons can be obligated to risk these goods. But since the distinction between a risk and a sacrifice is not neat, it may seem casuistic to allow that risking loss of certain goods can be obligatory while insisting that sacrificing them cannot be. Second, prior undertakings, whether in the form of explicit contracts or in that of the expectations springing from familial ties and friendship, can increase the degree of risk a person can be obligated to bear. Again, the suggestion is that nothing precludes raising the stakes to out-and-out sacrifice of the goods conferred by inalienable rights.

The foundation of this line of argument is the thought that, natural obligations to humanity-at-large aside, promises can surely create obligations to sacrifice anything. A promise can unequivocally specify repudiation, not risk, of a fundamental good. Also, while doubts can be raised about precisely which obligations are entailed by vague undertakings like military enlistment and parenthood, a straightforward promise to relinquish a particular good in appropriate circumstances generates an obligation to make the mentioned sacrifice if anything can. Thus, the critical test for the four inalienable rights I have proposed is whether promises to sacrifice the objects of these rights bind.

Ordinarily, we expect people to fulfill their promises for no other reason than that they have promised. However, we do not regard all promisory utterances as binding. A person who makes a promise under duress is not required to execute it; a person who promises to do something utterly fantastic is taken to be joking; and a person who promises to perform a vicious action does not transmute vice into duty. Though promises to sacrifice the objects of inalienable rights need not be extorted, wild, or evil, they bear a morally telling resemblance to these paradigmatic cases of nonbinding promisory utterance.

The typical situation in which a person might agree to sacrifice his life, personal liberty, sensory equilibrium, or allotment of basic necessities is a crisis. Battlefields, hospitals, and natural disasters supply familiar occasions for these sacrifices. In these contexts, critical interests are often jeopardized, and immediate action is imperative if terrible affliction is to be averted or if an important cause is to be salvaged.

Yet, self-sacrificial pledges made to contend with such dire emergencies are not accepted at face value. Unless the promisor is known to be exceptionally virtuous or profoundly devoted to the anticipated beneficiaries or the cause his sacrifice will serve, promisees are apt to be skeptical that he will fulfill his promise. Whereas we usually need no guarantee of a promisor's reliability beyond assurances that he is not generally dishonorable or vicious, we seek evidence of remarkable virtue or special attachments before trusting a promisor to give up the object of any of the four inalienable rights. An example will help to bring out why this dubious attitude is warranted.

Suppose an infantry platoon, surrounded and pinned down by enemy fire as night begins to fall and in imminent danger of being wiped out, hastily adopts a plan to create a diversion. One soldier, by breaking out alone, is to act as a decoy sacrificing her life to shield the others' escape. Someone volunteers for the suicidal assignment, and the troops set out as darkness comes. This scenario exhibits two morally questionable features: 1) the soldiers are invited to agree to perform an action which they are uncertain of their ability to do, and 2) the volunteer commits herself to a devastating and irremediable action but is given no time to reconsider. Though military training may inculcate fanatical hatred of the enemy along with a sense of mutual loyalty among fellow soldiers, a preparation that may steel the volunteer for her mission, most soldiers have no combat experience which would justify their affirming themselves to be reliable in the role of martyr. Moreover, since the indoctrination to which soldiers are subjected may prompt them to pledge their lives rashly, the fact that the volunteer must proceed immediately further compromises her promise. The other members of the platoon may have no alternative but to depend on the volunteer. Still, it is clear that their hopes must rest on the mock courage engendered in boot camp, rather than on normal scruples about fulfilling obligations created by legitimate promises.

Concerns about pressures that may unduly influence a decision as well as about the need for time to reflect on the commitment being considered are sometimes codified in legal waiting periods. Persons are, for example, required to hesitate before getting married and before getting sterilized. If decisions of this sort are provisional until an interval has elapsed, it is hard to see how promises to give up such essential goods as life, personal liberty, benign treatment, and satisfaction of basic needs could go into effect instantaneously. In fact, when it seems as if this kind of promise might bind the promisor immediately, supplementary considerations like the press of events and the duty not to harm others account for this impression. Nevertheless, since emergency conditions cannot curtail the promisor's need for time to think, these circumstances make solicitation of these promises illegitimate. Moreover, when trusting in the fulfillment of an improperly elicited promise foists on the promisor responsibility for serious harms consequent upon his reneging, promisees compound the wrong done the hapless promisor by giving credence to his word.

Although crises readily come to mind as situations that call forth major self-sacrifices, it is possible to imagine circumstances in which these sacrifices would be appropriate but not urgent. A society that permitted slavery might afford opportunities for free persons to sacrifice their personal liberty by trading places with slaves who wanted to be free. It might be customary in such a society for nonchattels who wished to liberate slaves to conclude arrangements for exchanging places which would be executed after a fixed waiting period. Slaves would understand that these agreements remained tentative until they were finalized, and free persons would understand that they could change their minds at any time prior to finalization. Assuming that it would be supererogatory for a stranger to substitute herself for a slave in the absence of any agreement to do so, would a free person's pledge reduce this supererogatory sacrifice to an obligation?

A promise to die, to submit to slavery, to endure agonizing pain, or to suffer severe deprivation for the sake of another person can be a promise to make a permissible gesture. But though the intended action is not necessarily wrong, such sacrifices are not morally indifferent, for they destroy, confine, or derange an autonomous participant in moral interaction. Promises to do evil are nugatory partly because of the harm their fulfillment would inflict on the victims of the promised evil and partly because fulfilling them would be degrading to the promisor. Promises to sacrifice the objects of inalienable rights present a more complicated moral picture. Aiming to bring about a great good for at least one other person but at grievous cost to the promisor, these promises appear to tie a benefactor to a beneficiary (the promisee need not be the beneficiary, but there must be a beneficiary for such a sacrifice to be appropriate), though it is not obvious in what this bond consists.

An ordinary promise selects an action that is simply permissible and transforms it into an obligation the promisor owes to the promisee. Inasmuch as a promise to sacrifice life, personal liberty, freedom from acute pain, or access to basic necessities altruistically must benefit someone who has standing as the prospective beneficiary, it is clear that the promisor would do wrong if she made the promised sacrifice but arbitrarily contrived for it to benefit someone other than the person named in the promise. In my hypothetical slave society, a free person who agreed to emancipate a particular slave would violate the terms of her agreement if she enslaved herself in exchange for some other slave's freedom. Thus, this type of promise is not devoid of moral force. Whereas a promise of wickedness effects no moral bond linking the promisor with anyone else, a promise of a permissible sacrifice commits the promisor to a particular beneficiary or group of beneficiaries.

This bond, however, would be impossible if it presupposed an obligatory sacrifice owed to the promisee. For regardless of the nobility of an individual's purpose, sacrificing the object of an inalienable right is necessarily degrading. Many experiences—sexual intercourse is a case in point—are degrading or not depending on whether a person consents to them. In contradistinction, the degradation of losing the object of an inalienable right is not dispelled by the victim's willingness to suffer this loss. The response typically evoked by altruistic sacrifices of these goods combines awe for the hero's fortitude and horror at what she has undergone. Though this horror may spring in part from vicarious fear, the fear would be nonsensical if not for a well-founded revulsion at the hero's degraded condition. Wretched if not altogether destroyed, this individual has sacrificed her autonomy and, with it, her capacity to renew or change her decision. Having renounced the basis of her dignity, she becomes her own helpless and pitiable victim.

Because sacrificing the object of an inalienable right necessarily degrades the right-holder—by definition, he concedes a prerequisite for moral agency—a person's promising to die, to enslave himself, to suffer acute pain, or to do without supplies of essential commodities to benefit another person cannot convert these supererogatory gestures into obligatory ones. Just as a religious martyr's bond to a deity does not make her submission to torture and death any less supererogatory, a promisor's bond to a beneficiary does not reduce the supererogatory sacrifice of a good conferred by an inalienable right to routine obligation fulfillment. Thus, an altruistic promise to sacrifice the object of an inalienable right binds the promisor only to a designated beneficiary; it does not bind him to make the sacrifice.

Mistrust is a reasonable response to a promise to sacrifice a good conferred by an inalienable right, for these promises do not bind the promisor in the usual way. Since promises to sacrifice life, personal liberty, freedom from acute pain, or access to basic necessities do not obligate the promisor to forgo these goods, the promisee is not entitled to demand these sacrifices. Lacking any moral leverage to persuade the promisor to carry out his intentions, the promisee is obliged to rely on the promisor's inclination to make a supererogatory sacrifice. Since dread and self-interest are likely to shake the promisor's resolve even if he is extraordinarily virtuous or profoundly committed to achieving an end, it would be Pollyannaish to expect the sacrifice from a normally kind and generous stranger.

7. Personal Worth and Personal Codes

I have argued that there are at least four rights with objects providing crucial support for moral agency. Three of these rights protect the individual agent—his life and two primary components of his well-being. The fourth, the right to personal liberty, directly protects his ability to exercise moral agency. Each of these rights sustains the individual's ability to function as a moral agent by contributing to a minimal level of physical and psychological equilibrium. A person may have embraced a moral system and may generally uphold it; however, violations of any of these four rights, in reducing the individual to a degraded state and his desire to be released from it, suppress the principled sense of responsibility that would ordinarily guide his conduct.

Now, someone might concede that these rights are vital to moral agency yet insist that sacrificing their objects is not invariably supererogatory. No doubt, persons are rarely obligated to sacrifice these goods, the argument goes; nevertheless, persons can be obligated to sacrifice them, as the remorse of parents who fail to save their children or the despair of resistance fighters who put themselves above their homeland shows. Different persons reflecting on this question are struck by different examples, but many persons are convinced that their principles could require them to die, to submit to coercion, to endure acute pain, or to suffer severe deprivation for altruistic reasons. It is not my contention that these judgments are aberrant or that they are distorted. Nevertheless, I would urge that these convictions, while normative, do not fall within the domain of morality.

Not everything that a person ought to do is morally required, though nothing that a person ought to do is immoral. Easily mistaken for moral dicta are the imperatives of personal codes. These codes embody personal ideals which capture different conceptions of what kind of person is most admirable and what kind of life is most worth living. A personal ideal lists and ranks values like the following: cultivation of a talent, advocacy of a cause, rich emotional associations, and service to humanity. No evil pursuits can be included in a personal ideal—which pursuits are worthwhile is not simply a matter of individual proclivity—but persons are free to order and weight desiderata as they please. Odd as it may be, there is nothing immoral in a person's opting to become a recluse in order to dedicate herself to composing piano rags. Except for the proviso that morality rules out wicked personal ideals and may restrict a person's freedom to act on a revised ideal once he has made commitments to others, a person's aspirations may be utterly idiosyncratic. Neither the choice of an ideal nor the fervor with which it is pursued is dictated by morality.

What differentiates a personal code from a moral system is the nonuniversalizability of the former. Two people could be endowed with similar abilities and find themselves in comparable circumstances and yet choose incompatible ideals. One might, for example, elect easy success while the other seeks challenges and courts defeat. Still, neither would be justified in condemning the other's course since both act within the confines of moral permissibility. Despite this moral latitude, however, these individuals might be severely disappointed in themselves. Whatever a person's standards, he may shrink from opportunities to test himself or perform poorly in the event. For these failings, because they pose obstacles to self-respect, a person may justifiably castigate himself.

A person cannot respect himself if he and his life diverge radically from his conception of a good person and a good life. Though no one is morally required to embrace a personal ideal or to strive to achieve it, self-respect is a good which few would willingly forswear. Consequently, persons view the dictates of their personal codes as mandatory and have reason to remonstrate with themselves to correct their faults as measured by their ideals.

Still, personal ideals are not uniformly demanding. One person's uncompromisable standard or goal is another's quixotic fancy; conversely, one person's sensible balance is another's mediocrity. Beyond this difference in difficulty of achievement, personal ideals vary in their complexity. Some concentrate heavily on one supreme value, whereas others blend a wide range of values. These variations account for the discrepancies among intuitions regarding self-sacrifice. Some people think that they must be prepared to rise to certain occasions, that anything less than heroism and munificence is sometimes contemptible. Others who consider humankind weak and this ideal cruelly unrealistic reject self-denial as a fair criterion of decency. And still others regard extreme self-sacrifice as misguided because they view the plenitude of life as capable of compensating for any misfortune. Thus, different personal ideals and the codes of conduct derived from them may dictate sacrifice of the objects of inalienable rights for different reasons or not at all.

For individuals whose personal codes could require altruistic sacrifices of life, personal liberty, freedom from pain, or access to basic necessities, these sacrifices may well seem obligatory. Inasmuch as self-respect is highly desirable and persons must follow their personal codes in order to secure this good, their conflation of the dictates of their personal codes with moral obligation is not surprising. From the standpoint of moral psychology, too, it is understandable that persons would not regard any sacrifices of the objects of inalienable rights required by their respective personal codes as morally superlative. Here, altruism is powerfully seconded by the self-interested desire for self-respect. Yet, the conclusion that these sacrifices are obligatory is unsound. Since persons are not morally bound to pursue self-respect and since a person's disposition to make a sacrifice does not trivialize its moral stature unless it has ignoble sources, the conviction that a sacrifice of the object of an inalienable right is morally mandatory confuses morality with individual ideals.

Fortunately, there is a corrective for the misapprehensions spawned by exalted personal codes. Persons who would declare themselves duty-bound to make some terrible sacrifice and who would condemn themselves for flinching in the face of doing their ostensible duty may also, for the sake of consistency, insist that others would have the same duty in the same situation. Still, they are usually reluctant to add that they would despise anyone if he failed to discharge this duty. Persons with high ideals hold themselves to rigid standards they do not apply to others; where they find no excuse for their own misdeeds, they see nothing for others to expiate. Whether because they imagine themselves to be superior persons or because they are tolerant of human diversity, they are not prepared to universalize these forms of self-sacrifice as a basis for moral blame. But, if these sacrifices were obligatory, exculpating cowardice or selfishness on the part of the sacrificer would do a catastrophic disservice to the rightful beneficiary of the sacrifice. Though persons who altruistically sacrifice the object of an inalienable right may modestly deprecate their conduct as mere obligation fulfillment, their refusal to demand equal virtue from others shows that they do not hold such action to be morally compulsory.

That a personal code may prescribe altruistic sacrifice of an adherent's life, personal liberty, deliverance from pain, or access to basic necessities explains how persons can firmly believe themselves to be obligated to make such sacrifices without its following that moral systems must impose equivalent prescriptions. Since persons are different, they espouse different personal ideals and personal codes to match. If a single personal code which exacted sacrifices of the objects of inalienable rights suited everyone or if all personal codes exacted the same sacrifices, personal codes would collapse into morality. In that case, the reasons for rejecting self-defeating moral systems would transfer to the offending personal code (or codes).[12] However, because personal codes are neither universal nor universalizable, they can require self-sacrificial action that would render a moral system self-defeating if it required identical conduct.

At this point, it might be observed that personal codes could obviate the need for morality. If everyone adopts a personal code, social relations could be ordered in accordance with this plurality of personal codes. Since individuals could dispense with morality, worries about self-defeating moral systems would vanish. Although this is much too large an issue to explore fully in the present context, it is necessary to sketch the limitations of personal codes.

Most important, personal codes must operate in the interstices of moral systems. Only where morality declares at least two options permissible and none required can a personal code take over an issue and legislate. But, it might be asked, why not place all questions about norms under the aegis of personal codes? Roughly, this arrangement is unsatisfactory because people can espouse personal ideals that are injurious to others, for example, the macho male, and inimical to social cooperation, for example, the criminal mastermind. Unless prescriptions derived from these deficient ideals are somehow ruled out, personal codes cannot be expected to harmonize and provide a workable basis for interpersonal relations. In effect, universal moral dicta censor the pernicious elements from personal codes. Moreover, a community relying exclusively on personal codes to govern social intercourse would at least be obliged to introduce an enabling moral precept which would obligate each individual to subscribe to an admissible personal code. Otherwise, persons could refuse to regulate their conduct in any way, and chaos could prevail with the assent of the community's normative system.

Without moral strictures and supports, personal codes could range over a spectrum so broad that they would fail to realize any ordering of social relations. However, provided that these codes are confined to supplementing morality, the variety of personal codes has highly desirable practical consequences. Generally, it ensures that persons will assume a wide assortment of complementary, though sometimes antagonistic, social roles. The interaction of persons following diverse personal codes contributes to social vitality. More narrowly, this diversity can enable individuals confronting crises to achieve more felicific outcomes than would otherwise be possible. Especially in the fearsome situations in which moral systems are necessarily mute, this potential for coordination among personal codes can make the difference between a riotous, counterproductive response and cooperation that minimizes harm. Some situations call for self-sacrifice destructive of moral agency, and personal codes can prescribe it though moral systems cannot.

4

Inalienable Rights and the Foundations of Moral Interaction

A moral system that recognizes rights to life, personal liberty, benign treatment, and satisfaction of basic needs must classify the four of them as rights that cannot be renounced conscientiously and therefore as strong candidates for inalienable rights. By permitting conscientious renunciation of these rights, a code of conduct would expose its self-defeating potential and would provide a decisive reason for rejecting it. Yet, there seems to be an intermediary position for moral systems to take. Instead of inalienable claim rights or conscientiously alienable ones, a moral system could recognize claim rights with respect to life, personal liberty, benign treatment, and satisfaction of basic needs that could be renounced solely by fiat. Since renunciation by fiat puts a universal simple permission regarding the object of the spurned claim right in the place of that claim right, this measure can create no self-defeating obligations. It is worth noting, however, that the original right-holder's competitive liberty to try to get or to keep his life, personal liberty, well-being, or basic necessities would be inalienable since renunciation of this liberty would obligate the right-holder to allow others to use this object as they please.[1] Thus, moral systems appear to have two alternatives to recognizing inalienable claim rights: they could recognize partially alienable claim rights, or they could dispense with claim rights altogether and recognize inalienable liberties. Inasmuch as it is undeniable that abridgment of inalienable rights is sometimes permissible, it is necessary to ask whether moral systems could extend this concession and regard killing, subjugation, torture, and deprivation as generally permissible, provided that the victims are entitled to defend themselves.

1. Rescission by Design

A moral system that substituted partially alienable claim rights or inalienable liberties for inalienable claim rights would satisfy the requirement that moral systems not be self-defeating. This negative criterion of adequacy states that moral systems must not prescribe, though they may permit, termination of adherence to their prescriptions. A moral system countenancing conscientious renunciation of the rights to life, personal liberty, benign treatment, and satisfaction of basic needs or alienation of a congruent set of liberties would allow persons to incur obligations to submit to attacks on these vital goods. Thus, it would be capable of self-defeating prescriptions.

But a moral system recognizing claim rights that could only be renounced by fiat or inalienable liberties could never authorize right-holders to obligate themselves to refrain from trying to deter or repulse such onslaughts.[2] A person who has a liberty with respect to some good lacks the security a right would afford since others may contend with him for this good; however, unlike a person who has neither a right nor a liberty, he enjoys the option of contesting attempts to deprive him of the object of his liberty. Because of this difference, a moral system conferring partially alienable claim rights or inalienable liberties instead of inalienable rights cannot be routinely discarded for its capacity to generate self-defeating prescriptions.

Still, the characterization of inalienable rights as ones with objects that are necessary for moral agency and that can only be sacrificed supererogatorily might seem to rule out any weaker mode of protection. After all, it would be puzzling if the objects of these rights were so central to persons' stature as moral agents that no one could be obligated to relinquish them and yet anyone could try to wrest them from right-holders. The importance of these goods seems to dictate a commensurately strong form of moral protection for them.

Nevertheless, the analysis of inalienability given so far does not decide the question of whether goods screened from obligatory sacrifice must be protected by claim rights or liberties. Both an exclusive entitlement to enjoy these goods and an entitlement to compete to retain (or obtain) them are compatible with the claim that the benefits specified are not amenable to obligatory sacrifice. A liberty, it must be admitted, introduces a morally condoned risk that the right-holder will lose a critically important good he has struggled to keep, but it does not oblige right-holders to confront fearsome overtures passively. Moreover, as with the protection provided by claim rights, the protection of liberties does not exclude supererogatory sacrifice of the relevant good since a person could choose not to counter a challenge to his enjoyment of it.

Once it is evident that neither the requirement that moral systems not be self-defeating nor the criteria for identifying rights which are not conscientiously renounceable can establish that inalienable rights must be claim rights rather than liberties, a last-resort appeal might be made to common sense. If persons were morally permitted to kill, enslave, torture, and snatch basic necessities from one another, what could they be morally prohibited from doing or morally constrained to do? And if no moral proscriptions or prescriptions were binding, could any moral system be said to be governing interpersonal relations? In short, Hobbes's portrayal of a state of nature in which each individual is free to do whatever he thinks best to advance his interests is, as Hobbes himself insists, an amoral vision.[3]

This intuitive argument, though sound as far as it goes, fails to penetrate to an explanation of the impossibility of inalienable liberties. Hobbes contends that unchanneled egoism compels persons to act on a policy of wary but ambitious self-aggrandizement that leaves everyone worse off than they would be if they cooperated to implement restrictive norms. On Hobbes's view, persons must give up their original liberty in order to escape their wretched condition.[4] Thus, Hobbes assumes that the liberties in question must be transmutable into the duties summed up in the golden rule on the grounds that their permanence would block any prospect of civilizing egoism.

Unlike Hobbes, however, I have not relied on egoistic premises to account for inalienable rights.[5] Without this foundation, to rest my case for the impossibility of inalienable liberties on an appeal to the misery they would engender would be tantamount to resting content with a wholly ad hoc dismissal of these liberties. But since neither the role in moral systems I have assigned to inalienable rights nor the criteria for inalienable rights I have defended defeats the possibility of inalienable liberties, my theory of inalienable rights would be inconclusive and seriously defective without an account of why no moral system could include these liberties. For it is plain that inalienable liberties would be pernicious: they would instate a morality we might aptly label gladiatorial.

In arguing that the proposed inalienable liberties are impossible, I shall employ the idea of rescission by design. In contrast to a self-defeating moral system which sustains moral interaction while harboring a capacity to terminate it, a moral system that suffers from rescission by design is one that forecloses the possibility of moral interaction by generating moral relations incompatible with moral compliance. Whereas a self-defeating moral system imitates the impact of lethal natural disasters by prescribing the destruction of moral agency, a self-rescinding moral system internalizes the dynamic of catastrophe by issuing permissions or prescriptions which themselves license departure from normal moral constraints. Just as *in extremis* conditions can pressure moral communities to the breaking point, wayward moral direction can sabotage conscientious

Foundations of Moral Interaction

adherence. Admittedly, a moral system that prescribes, proscribes, or permits conduct creating a moral environment which blocks moral interaction may produce less spectacularly cataclysmic results than a self-defeating moral system might—agents may be left paranoid and addled, rather than agonized or dying—but a self-rescinding moral system would be no more adequate as a guide to conduct.

The burden of the ensuing sections will be that inalienable liberties with respect to life, personal liberty, benign treatment, and satisfaction of basic needs are impossible because any moral system containing them would be self-rescinding. In recognizing inalienable liberties, I shall contend, a moral system releases its adherents from the obligation to represent themselves honestly, generates a system of impenetrable deceit, and thereby confounds moral agency. If this line of argument is correct, not only are the goods which are objects of inalienable rights necessary for moral agency, but also inalienable claim rights themselves are. In addition to the impossibility of inalienable liberties, then, it follows that renouncing the rights to life, personal liberty, benign treatment, and satisfaction of basic needs by fiat, in other words, disowning exclusive title to a good conferred by one of these rights while retaining a liberty with respect to that good, must be impossible.[6] However unlikely it might be that everyone would choose to renounce these rights by fiat, the possibility is sufficient to reject any moral system which could allow this state of affairs to transpire.[7] For delayed, piecemeal rescission by design is unacceptable for the same reasons that self-defeatism and overt rescission by design are.

2. Inalienable Liberties

Substituting inalienable liberties for inalienable rights is not equivalent to the wrong of violating inalienable rights. Inalienable liberties permit persons to try to kill, subjugate, torture, and deprive one another of basic necessities and concomitantly permit persons to defend themselves against these attacks. Thus, if a person succeeds in enslaving someone, she does not wrong her chattel; contrariwise, if the slave manages to escape, she does not wrong her master. This gladiatorial morality declares competition for the goods of life, personal liberty, freedom from pain, and access to basic necessities morally legitimate. Accordingly, it serves notice that no one would consider himself obligated to honor any claim to noninterference or aid with respect to these goods, and it carries an implicit threat of attacks on these goods. Persons who have only inalienable liberties, then, are exposed to insupportable afflictions but are not necessarily enduring any. Insofar as persons with inalienable liberties do not successfully compete to kill, subjugate, torture, or otherwise degrade their fellows, the victims are not relieved of their status as moral agents.[8] Yet, they are obliged to rely on their ability to defend and promote their most fundamental interests rather than on an entitlement to a core of security.

To qualify for inalienable liberties, an individual must share with us the same basic purposes, capacities, and vulnerabilities. Like us, she must value her life, must wish to control the direction it takes, must suffer if pained, and must require sustenance and shelter from unpropitious environmental conditions for survival. If she did not resemble us in these ways, there would be no reason to grant her permission to mount defenses against attacks on her life, personal liberty, freedom from pain, or access to basic necessities. Still, by hypothesis, she lacks firm moral protection answering to these interests. Inalienable liberties with respect to life, coercion, acute pain, and basic necessities would render aggression and indifference to suffering, on the one hand, and self-defense and pursuit of well-being, on the other, simply permissible. Exercising these competitive liberties would be on a par with familiar competitive activities like trying to get a job or trying to win a tennis match. Regarded as morally neutral, assault and deliberate deprivation would not be uncommon in a society recognizing only inalienable liberties despite the importance to agents of avoiding these harms.

Against this claim, it might be urged that inalienable rights have little effect on conduct and therefore that the elimination of these moral guarantees would not appreciably increase the probability of aggression or refusal to give aid. This contention might be understood in any of several ways. The idea could be that human psychology would inhibit agents from exercising these liberties. Either various motivational principles would combine to damp violence and meanness, or considerations of self-interest would largely replicate the curbs of inalienable rights. Alternatively, it might be thought that social pressure or legal sanctions might check aggression and indifference to others despite the moral neutrality of these interpersonal modalities. Finally, it might be maintained that moral principles anterior to inalienable liberties would constrain their exercise, thus mitigating the practical impact of these permissions.

Taking the last of these interpretations first, I shall assume that the moral force of inalienable liberties is not neutralized by independent moral considerations.[9] Though many moral reasons undeniably militate against exercising competitive liberties regarding life, coercion, benign treatment, and satisfaction of basic needs, the point of asking whether inalienable liberties would be admissible is to see whether morally unrestricted competition over the objects of these liberties would undermine moral interaction. We can learn nothing about the outer limits of possible simple permissions if we advert to superseding duties to close off those permissions before exploring their effects on moral relations. If these permissions turn out to do no damage to moral interaction, this discovery might lead us to question the duties that we now suppose would preempt these liberties.

Still, human psychology might minimize the hazards of accepting inalienable liberties. If people are naturally averse to attacking their fellows and to withholding essential goods from them, morality merely affirms the inevitable in prohibiting these types of treatment. Consequently, declaring them simply permissible would not invert these sociable dispositions. However, no one believes that morality is simply a codification and celebration of human psychology. Moral education would be unnecessary if morality fit human nature this neatly. And it is precisely because our psychology harbors malign as well as fine impulses that human affairs need moral regulation. It is reasonable, therefore, to conjecture that persons would avail themselves of inalienable liberties in much the same way as they normally avail themselves of other simple permissions.

Taking a walk, buying a pet, watching television, and dining at a restaurant are all morally neutral activities. Not everyone does them, and no one does them all the time. But no widespread and strong disinclination to do them prevails; doing them is not morally objectionable; and, as a result, many people are quite likely to do them sometime. Only if a morally indifferent activity requires a special taste or talent (cultivating orchids, for instance), exceptional wealth (collecting old masters, for instance), or other atypical inclinations or resources is it the case that simply permissible conduct nevertheless remains rare. Accordingly, aggression and deprivation would be commonplace in a community that credited only inalienable liberties since exercising these liberties calls upon widely distributed traits which can be vented in countless circumstances. Neither hostility nor the means of expressing hostility through violence or refusal to give aid is sufficiently exotic to warrant a pacific vision of social relations based on inalienable liberties.

At this point, someone might interject that an action can be morally permissible and yet be socially frowned upon (picking your nose) or legally sanctioned (smoking marijuana). Despite their moral indifference it might be observed, uncouth forms of behavior can be effectively repressed through customary or institutional enforcement. Surely, the pugnacity and callousness underlying exercise of inalienable liberties are offensive, even if they are not immoral.

Though peer pressure and legal penalties successfully induce people to project conventional public images, these forces are strikingly ineffectual in rooting out secret indulgence. When norms altogether lack moral backing, close scrutiny often reveals social conformity to be an apparent phenomenon. In private, people take advantage of simple permissions. If this view of amoral conventions is accurate, the suggestion that exercising inalienable liberties might be shunned in polite society or prohibited by law is nothing more than a prescription for driving these activities underground. Morally ratified standards of conduct tend to endure and to gain adherents; arbitrary rules tend to be flouted on the sly. For my present purposes, the difference between open and concealed violence is immaterial. In neither case is the exercise of inalienable liberties scotched.

Persons who have only inalienable liberties have reason to anticipate the worst from others. Because no one is entitled to minimal respect and concern on anyone else's part, each must realize that in principle others would not hesitate to degrade, injure, or kill her. Though an individual may never have been victimized, she cannot be confident that her immunity will last. Admittedly, inalienable claim rights do not ensure perfect compliance. Yet, they do confine the likelihood of violations to a range of familiar and readily recognizable circumstances which people can by and large take care to avoid. In contrast armed only with inalienable liberties, persons cannot use their knowledge of the stress points in the moral network to predict danger. While a person can surmise that her present tenuous safety is due to the fact that those who might engage her in conflict have neither a reason nor an inclination to afflict her and she can speculate about what might provoke them to attack, their conduct is bound to remain a moral conundrum. Since she has only liberties, she must assume that whatever treatment she receives at the hands of her fellows is independent of her status or the propriety of her behavior. That is, she cannot take others' non-aggression as an acknowledgment that she deserves to be left unmolested, and she cannot take their assaults, should they occur, as punishments for her transgressions against them or as regrettable responses to intractable circumstances. The realm of mutual respect and responsibility constituted by inalienable claim rights has been abandoned. People must regard one another with apprehension, if not downright terror.

Persons, then, would confront one another in

roughly the same way as Californians unable to move away confront the San Andreas fault. This geological time bomb is indifferent to the humanity of the residents of California and poses a constant threat of an earthquake. Similarly, in acknowledging inalienable liberties, a society objectifies its members and thereby compels all of them to live in dread of aggressive campaigns. For members of a society of this sort, failed defenses are like natural disasters: they are bad for the victims, but no one is to blame. As a result, persons who have inalienable liberties are justified in adopting the same defensive stance toward their compatriots as Californians might appropriately adopt with respect to the San Andreas fault. Certainly, every effort is made to understand this geological phenomenon in order to learn to predict slippages and thus to minimize damage in the event of an earthquake, and presumably everyone would embrace a safe way to engineer the immobility of the fault if one could be found. Likewise, it is appropriate for persons deprived of a basic measure of security to seek regularities in one another's conduct in order to anticipate aggression, and it is appropriate for them to manipulate one another in order to forestall aggression. For these people cannot afford to be daunted by their adversaries' humanity any more than Californians can afford to anthropomorphize the San Andreas fault.

The primary consideration for an individual in choosing principles of action under these conditions is properly self-defense. Because she lacks guarantees of her safety, she is vulnerable to injuries that can destroy or temporarily disrupt her ability to function rationally. She is in a doubly dangerous predicament. On the one hand, she—more than anyone else—needs to be in command of her faculties in order to protect herself; on the other hand, she—more than anyone else—is subject to losing control over her conduct as a result of the incursions or neglect of others. Assuming that there is no hope of converting inalienable liberties into claim rights, it is reasonable for a person to adopt the following egoistic policy in dealings with other members of her society: I may do whatever in my judgment is most likely to stifle competition for the objects of

Foundations of Moral Interaction 93

my inalienable liberties, and, if preventive tactics fail, I may do whatever in my judgment will crush the attack or reduce the harm I suffer. If personal security is not morally assured yet remains a preeminent desideratum for individuals, self-protection can never cease to be an urgent consideration. It befits the predicament, then, that ordinary moral principles should be suspended in deference to this superordinate preoccupation, and that defensive egoism should become a widely favored arbiter of individual conduct.

3. Justifying Self-interested Deceit

Though the suggestion that persons who are radically and inescapably insecure are justified in espousing unrestricted defensive egoism is intuitively plausible, I shall not argue this point further. Since my critique of inalienable liberties will depend entirely on the weaker contention that persons with inalienable liberties would have no duty not to conduct themselves deceptively, I shall confine my argument for defensive egoism to the narrower claim that morality cannot hold a person to honesty when his life, personal liberty, benign treatment, and access to basic necessities are in jeopardy.

The obligation to act nondeceitfully is, of course, a prima facie obligation which countenances quite a few exceptions. The least controversial and the most common justifications for unabashed deceit invoke the good of other persons: honesty would have needlessly injured them. But self-interested deceit is sometimes justified, too. In order to highlight our everyday beliefs about justifiable self-interested deceit, it is useful to contemplate the relations that would obtain between masters and their chattels in a society condoning slavery.

According to the public morality of such a society, no slave would have a right not to be killed although slave owners would have rights not to have their property destroyed. Thus, the owner of a slave would have a right to kill the slave, and the prohibition on others' killing the slave would represent an obligation to the owner, not an obligation to the slave. Needless to say, slaves would be required to submit to their masters' wishes. Since slave owners would enjoy a right to obedience from their slaves, no slave would have a right not to be forced to execute another's dictates. Finally, although prudent masters would minimize the pain they inflicted on their slaves and would provide for their slaves' basic needs, the slaves would not have a right to such care, nor would they have a right to protect themselves or to provide basic necessities for themselves through entrepreneurial undertakings. Slaves would be completely at the mercy of their masters.

It is easy to conceive of situations in which deceitful conduct on the part of a slave would be permissible. A slave who might contrive to make her thwarting of her owner's attempt to kill her appear to be something other than an act of defiance could not be faulted. A slave who was being punished for some petty offense by a starvation diet would be justified in stealing food if she had the opportunity to do so without getting caught. A slave who feigned love and respect for her master while nursing hatred and plans for escape or revolt would engage in justifiable deceit. Indeed, it is hard to think of a form of duplicity that a slave definitely could not justify practicing against her master under the assumed conditions. A docile persona may rightfully conceal a slave's self-protective strategies, whether these schemes are aimed at limited and immediate benefits or at eventual liberation from bondage.

Even within the slave class, the obligation to engage in nondeceitful relations would be weakened. Slaves would not be free to exercise the powers over one another which their masters appropriated exclusively for themselves, yet the broader social context would probably foment distrust among them. The main justification for deceit within the slave class would be the presence of unknown informers within the group and the possibility that another slave would divulge an unguarded confidence in order to gain favor with the master. Considering the wretched position of the slaves, it would be

Foundations of Moral Interaction

heartless to excoriate those who, goaded by their masters, succumbed to the temptation to try to improve their lot through treachery.

Despite the moral position of the slaves, there is no reason to suppose that any similar moral breakdown would occur within the master class. Of course, a master surrounded by justifiably deceitful slaves might be disposed to conceive paranoiac fears as to the sincerity of her fellow slave owners, but such crises of trust need not be sufficiently frequent or widespread to sabotage moral relations among masters. The slave owners would secure for themselves what they would deny to their slaves, namely, inalienable rights.

The moral order of a society divided between masters and slaves is an incoherent one. The official morality imposes obligations of submission on slaves which no acceptable moral system can countenance. Consequently, slaves are, on any acceptable moral view, justified in refusing to fulfill these obligations. This refusal, whether in the direct form of open insubordination or in the oblique form of deceptive wiles, must be classified as self-defense. From the standpoint of a satisfactory moral system, slaves must be regarded as having inalienable liberties, at least. In effect, these liberties authorize slaves to act as if their owners, too, had only inalienable liberties and so to employ whatever preventive and evasive stratagems are least risky and most ready-to-hand. Specifically, they justify virtually unlimited duplicity. Even if we are prompted to insist that morality limits the ways in which slaves may avenge themselves—for example, torturing their masters or shackling them in turn may not be permissible—we resist the claim that duplicitous tactics would ever be barred. After all, deceit seems the least costly type of self-protection that slaves have at their disposal.

That compliance with the obligation to engage in nondeceitful interpersonal relations is morally dependent on secure inalienable rights is borne out by our convictions regarding various situations in which these rights are at risk. For example, once a person has been accused of a crime, her inalienable rights are in jeopardy. If she is convicted of the crime, her punishment will be a controlled and presumably commensurate infringement of one of her inalienable rights. Capital punishment infringes the right to life; imprisonment infringes the right to personal liberty; corporal punishment infringes the right to benign treatment; and fines attack the individual's ability to satisfy basic needs.[10] Since the threat of punishment for a crime is not equivalent to outright denial of a defendant's inalienable rights, being indicted does not free the accused individual to deploy any and all means of eluding conviction. Defendants are prohibited from obstructing justice by conspiring to conceal crimes or by implicating innocent parties. Still, our recognition of the right not to incriminate oneself embodies our conviction that a person cannot be obligated to cooperate in the abridgment of her own inalienable rights. Withholding information bearing on respect for others' rights is usually impermissible. Nevertheless, if a defendant is knowingly forthcoming with self-incriminatory evidence when she has not been granted immunity from prosecution, her conduct must be viewed as a supererogatory contribution to social stability and order.[11] Thus, ordinary morality makes a limited exception to the obligation to engage in nondeceitful relations for persons accused of crimes because we do not believe these individuals can be required to honor this obligation to the extent of attracting punitive infringements of their inalienable rights. The latitude in regard to deceit that we condone in the areas of justified warfare and espionage confirms this point.

   Now, it might be objected that conventional, twentieth-century Western morality does permit deception or a departure from full candor when a person's life, personal liberty, benign treatment, or access to basic necessities is threatened but that moral systems could conceivably withhold this permission. There could be a moral system permitting competition over the objects of inalienable liberties but exacting reverence for an authority who forbids all deception—call this the servile gladiatorial system—or there could be a moral system permitting these forms of competition but forbidding defensive du-

Foundations of Moral Interaction

plicity to those who had agreed to abstain from it—call this the chivalric gladiatorial system. Inhumane as these codes of conduct may seem, they are not self-evidently unacceptable.

The first point to notice about both of these moral systems is that they appeal to morally fortuitous elements to justify their honesty requirements. An authority or an agreement is imported into the moral system to give the idea that defensive deception could be prohibited to radically insecure individuals what credibility it has. If we ask, instead, whether people might simply believe themselves morally bound never to use deceptive subterfuges in self-defense, the attractions of honesty-enforcing gladiatorial systems dissipate.

Furthermore, the contemplated moral system would be more than usually unstable. Since persons would not know whether others were scrupulously observing the honesty dicta, and since the price of miscalculation in this regard would be devastating, the temptation to ignore their moral duty to represent themselves honestly would incessantly afflict the exponents of this moral system. Presumably, they would often yield to it. To counter this tendency, child-rearing practices might be devised to cultivate an enthusiasm for truth-telling capable of disciplining any proclivity toward self-preserving deceit. But whether or not this result could be achieved, it is highly doubtful that it would profit anyone to institute the requisite nurturing methods. Cleaving to honesty while viewing murder, subjugation, torture, and severe deprivation as simply permissible would evidence a bewildering infatuation with the niceties of moral interaction comparable to embracing a table etiquette so elaborate and refined that no food would ever be consumed.

Ordinarily, persons are obligated to confine their deceptive conduct to altruistic purposes if they engage in deceptive conduct that might be considered morally objectionable at all. Yet, because altruistically sacrificing any good secured by an inalienable right is supererogatory, right-holders cannot be morally required to act so as to allow others to deprive them of this good in pursuit of private or, for that matter, public ends. A person's adherence to the obligation to engage in nondeceitful interpersonal relations when a benefit associated with an inalienable right is at stake is tantamount to complicity in any harms others may inflict in taking advantage of his naivete. But no one can be obligated to divest himself, however circuitously, of his defenses against these misfortunes.

When inalienable rights are officially denied or only inalienable liberties are acknowledged, deception and honesty are converted into weapons in the defensive arsenal of the dispossessed. For, as we have seen, when these pitiable individuals are not actually under attack, they remain under protracted siege and may use their weapons to ameliorate their condition. If honesty can be morally mandatory only when persons are tolerably safe but inalienable liberties establish a social environment in which persons are never safe, the distinction between deceit which is permissible in view of a good reason and simply permissible deceit collapses. Since a good reason for deceit always obtains, invoking that reason is superfluous. And since by hypothesis it is not contemplated to change the condition which invariably provides this good reason, namely, instatement of inalienable liberties, defensive deceit can hardly be viewed as a regrettable exigency in unfortunate circumstances. In placing persons' most critical interests at risk and leaving them to their own devices to protect these interests, inalienable liberties reduce deceit and honesty to moral indifference.

4. Impenetrable Deceit

Violations of inalienable rights derange moral agency by permanently or temporarily hobbling the victim's sensitivity to others' concerns along with his commitment to a moral code. But inalienable liberties merely expose persons to the possibility of being reduced to this distraught condition. If these liberties negate moral agency, this result must be a secondary effect, that is, a consequence of the moral implications of recognizing inalienable liberties to the exclusion of inalienable claim rights. To see that moral agency could not survive if persons had only inalienable liberties, it is necessary to examine a social world in which a gladiatorial moral system permitting defensive deceit is in force.

This inquiry might be pursued from any of several perspectives. A transition from a society recognizing inalienable claim rights to one recognizing inalienable liberties or, the reverse, an exit from a society recognizing inalienable liberties could be envisioned. Better still, the internal viewpoint of a society which sees no alternative to gladiatorial morality could be conceived. Since the first two approaches bring into play our conditioned aversions to the gladiatorial conception of moral relations—we automatically assume persons would resist conversion to inalienable liberties and that they would welcome institution of inalienable claim rights—it is best to minimize the influence of these biases by exploring a world unequivocally committed to gladiatorial morality.

Plunging into a world governed by gladiatorial morality confronts us with a social system in which no one is morally resolved not to kill, subjugate, torture, and deprive others of basic necessities and in which aggressive schemes may be undertaken on any pretext. Deceit and honesty are therefore considered to be morally neutral means of prosecuting standing defensive ends. At this point, it is important to appreciate that, despite its many exceptions, the obligation to act nondeceitfully normally constrains our conduct sharply. There being multifarious forms of deceit, opportunities to mislead others and reasons for doing so constantly present themselves. Through verbal or nonverbal expression, the liar represents himself as believing propositions which he thinks are false, the hypocrite pretends to accept principles which he surreptitiously ignores in practice, and the shirker protests his innocence and blames others for what he has done. Thus, to be released from the obligation to engage in honest interpersonal relations is to be freed of one of our most pervasive moral strictures, and the changes resulting from removing all obstacles to deceit except the radically insecure individual's perception of his own defensive needs are likely to be profound.

Many philosophers have observed that the distinction between honesty and dishonesty can only be maintained in practice against a background of normally honest conduct. Kant claims that it would become impossible to make a promise if everyone were to adopt a policy of pretending to make a promise without any intention of fulfilling it whenever that strategy seemed convenient.[12] And A.I. Melden remarks, "Without the telling of the truth there can be no lying."[13] In one sense, this is all perfectly obvious. If we knew that promisors typically broke their promises, we would discount any promise we might receive. Also, if lying were as common as truth-telling, we would not believe anything we heard until it could be independently confirmed. Skepticism is undoubtedly the most rational attitude with which to meet an uncertain world. However, Kant, along with his followers, seems to have considered the prospect of general dishonesty more worrisome than this pragmatic conclusion suggests.

Regarding honesty and deceit as equally permissible isolates persons from one another and deprives them of an accurate idea of the social context in which they are obliged to act. Since neither shame nor guilt would attach to deceit, the signs that give us reason to suspect deception would never give anyone away. Having shed their tendency to become flustered when found out, people would masterfully employ techniques for dismissing such discoveries and for diverting their accusers. Thus, deceitful acts would instigate additional deceitful tactics aimed at finessing detection. An initial deception could then breed an endless, branching concatenation of deceptions, which would draw other persons into the web by the need to protect themselves. Unhesitant and skilled in deceitful practices, persons would never glimpse enough undeniable and suitably related cases of deception or honesty to begin deciphering their social environment.[14]

Under these circumstances, there would be no way to gain insight into persons' reasons for misleading others because reliable data would be unobtainable. All testimony would be untrustworthy. Consequently, no one would be able to anticipate deceit or, for that matter, to estimate the frequency of deceit. Deceit could be constant or sporadic; it could be undertaken purposively or on a whim; the perpetrators' motives could be malicious, benevolent, or simply self-interested. In the absence of solid information about what others were really doing coupled with explanations of why they were doing it, deceit would be unpredictable, as well as undetectable.

In a world of impenetrable deceit, a person's experience of her relations with other people would be confined to her apprehension of her associates' physical movements and professed versions of reality. Lies would be told, misleading schemes would be executed, but shreds of truth would intermittently surface, too. If an individual's acquaintances are clever, their conduct—the impression it makes along with their commentary on it—would be internally consistent. Indeed, the statements and actions of different individuals might sometimes seem to corroborate one another; however, this concurrence could just as well be taken as evidence of a conspiracy as proof of authenticity. Equally alarming, agents would often confront irreconcilably contradictory statements and behavior emanating from diverse sources. In sum, an agent in a society affirming deceit-permissive gladiatorial morality must cope with experience that is inherently dubious, often incoherent, but nonetheless incorrigible. All interpretations of interpersonal experience, including moral characterization and appraisal, would be foundationless.

Despite the unintelligibility of this social environment, persons would be obliged to make decisions and to act as best they could to secure their own interests and to pursue any other objectives they might have. Gladiatorial morality gives persons compelling reasons to avail themselves of deceitful machinations, but, in so doing, it levels the advantage the deceitful enjoy when they can count on others to be honest. Worse, it condemns persons to a social solipsism which renders planning nugatory. Blind to all but the surface pattern of events, persons would lack sufficient knowledge to set realistic long-range goals and to make steady progress toward them. However chancy we presently find coordinating our pursuit of complex and distant ends, the imponderables would proliferate astronomically if we suddenly lost all confidence in our perception of others' immediate motives and extended projects. Voiding the prohibition on deceit does not prevent persons from hoping to attain their various ends, but it does confine them to proceeding from moment to moment in what they suppose to be their chosen directions.

The world described above is probably sufficiently distressing to send anyone gladly to the refuge of obligatory sincerity and forthrightness, but the most serious implications of a deceit-ridden world have yet to be explored. So far, I have supposed that each perpetrator of deceit would know that she was deceiving others and each honest person would know that she was purveying the truth. Broadly, I have assumed that each individual would remain able to identify, describe, and evaluate her own acts, though not anyone else's. But, as I shall argue in the next section, this assumption is unsound.

5. Amoral Action and Enforced Irresponsibility

The underlying reason for Kant's overweening denunciation of deceit can be traced to an inextricable connection between moral agency and general compliance with the prohibition on deceit. A moral agent must be capable of choosing and following a code of conduct that takes into account the interests of other persons. Though a moral agent might elect an egoistic ethic that considers other persons only insofar as they may help or hinder him, a person does not qualify as a moral agent unless he is capable of opting instead to display respect and concern for his fellows. Persons are absolved of moral responsibility when they cannot control the effects of their conduct on others. Thus, the question of what would prevent individuals from realizing this capacity can be construed as the question of what would obviate the possibility of their responsibly undertaking to adhere to a system of precepts dictating mutual care and nonaggression. The dissociation that would develop not only between the individual and her acquaintances but also between the individual and her own conduct if inalienable liberties were recognized and deceit were not proscribed would preclude moral agency.

The first question we may raise about the predicament gladiatorial morality creates concerns the individual agent's ability to characterize her own conduct accurately. A moral agent must know what she is doing. By hypothesis, no one in a society governed by gladiatorial morality ever knows who is deceiving her or how she is being deceived. But can a person know whether her own actions are deceitful or forthright and, more generally, whether they are right or wrong?

Two connected problems suggest that persons could not recognize their own deceitful or honest conduct. Each participant in this social network must either blindly embrace rules of thumb for interpreting others' conduct—such as 'Believe every third brown-eyed person you encounter'—or must randomly classify information conveyed as deceptive or authentic. Whichever policy an individual adopts, it is accidental if her appraisal of any given action is correct. Conversely, when a person acts, she can never be justified in expecting anyone else to take her conduct for what it appears to be and cannot reasonably suppose that her attempted deceptions or her essays at honesty have succeeded. Since she is only her listener's second brown-eyed person but does not know what rule her listener is using and could not find out how her action fit with that rule anyway, her sincere warning of an enemy's plot will be ignored or viewed as a plot itself.

This dilemma is compounded by the fact that a systemically deceitful social world makes it impossible for an agent to follow up an act's long-range consequences. Any actor seeking to ascertain the consequences of her conduct would be obliged to subscribe to some explanatory theory of experienced events which would authorize her to assign causal connections between actions and subsequent occurrences. But at each step, an agent inquiring into the effects of her conduct would face impenetrable deceit. Indeed, since this individual's acquaintances would also be experiencing life through a veil of deceit, they would not know whether their testimony proved to be injurious or helpful. Thus, their testimony would be utterly worthless. It could be given sincerely but in fact mislead the inquirer, or it could be given deceitfully and do the same. Yet, even if it is given sincerely and in fact validates accurate conjectures, or if it is given deceitfully but happens to do the same, nonetheless the individual who has solicited others' help has no way of knowing what kind of response she is getting. For she can use neither the distinction between lying and inadvertently giving incorrect information nor the distinction between truth-telling and inadvertently giving correct information to prize open her perceptions.

Inasmuch as explanatory theories of human relations would have to be fabricated out of irremediable and boundless ignorance, persons would expect and would find consequences where there were none and would overlook consequences where they were to be found. A person may have greatly influenced the course of events and believe herself to have been impotent, or, the other way around, she may have been a mere cipher but believe her gesture to have been decisive. At any rate, such individuals would never know whether or not their theories were leading them astray. They would perceive sequences of events but would not understand their connections. If deceit and honesty were equally permissible, agents could not distinguish their own deceitful from their own honest conduct because they could not discern after the fact whether or not their audience had accepted the purport of their actions. Only an omniscient observer could make these discriminations.

At this juncture, someone might counter that I have neglected the actors' intentions. They may never know whether their plans have panned out, but they would know whether they intended to mislead anyone. As a result, they can evaluate themselves, though not their impact on the world. But how could intentions enter into a person's understanding of her conduct? Since by hypothesis deception is neither good nor bad in itself, intending to deceive will warrant neither approbation nor condemnation. If intentions are to figure in an actor's characterization of her action, it must be because of what she proposes to achieve through deception or forthrightness. Unfortunately, under the conditions posited, these intentions are likewise irrelevant.

Provided that the world is arranged so that good intentions are normally correlated with right conduct and bad intentions with wrong conduct and this is known to the participants, a person's intentions can legitimately enter into her judgments about her own conduct. She can praise or blame herself for both her intentions and her act, she can castigate herself for her bad intentions while exulting in the unexpectedly good results of her actions, or she can congratulate herself for her good intentions while regretting her act. However, when the world is constituted so that virtuous intentions are as likely, if not more likely, to yield disastrous results rather than desirable ones and vicious intentions are likely to produce contrary effects and it is impossible to ascertain the objective import of one's own action, good or bad intentions are indistinguishable. Since an impenetrable system of deception and honesty stymies prediction of the probable consequences of action, intentions of whatever sort must be presumed to produce randomly good and bad results and therefore must be viewed as morally neutral. Thus the fact that an actor intends to bring about a desirable objective cannot justify her in reaching a favorable or adverse judgment of her own intentions, nor could an omniscient observer exculpate or censure her on this basis.

With the presumption of honesty on the part of other persons negated but with no definite guidance about the forms of duplicity employed by others to replace it, persons would find it impossible to follow consequentialist rules. To illustrate, social intercourse would appear to a group of persons trying to uphold defensive egoism as a bewildering labyrinth of concealed motives, diversionary tactics, cross-purposes, misalliances, and the like. The general obfuscation effected by this state of affairs would prevent agents from gauging the consequences of their acts beyond each act's most immediate impact on themselves. Of course a person could realize that a sensation of pain was due to a pinprick. But, unable to comprehend indirect or future developments, individuals would be thwarted in their attempts to characterize their conduct as self-interested or self-destructive. Conduct yielding prompt advantages might well have catastrophic, but unassignable circuitous or delayed consequences for the actor. Feeling sated after a large and tasty meal, a person would classify eating it as self-interested. But, since the food could have been poisoned and may yet have its effect, it is doubtful that this classification is warranted. Only if nothing ever went wrong could an agent surmise that she must have been successfully following her egoistic precept. If misfortunes befell her, she could not discover their causes. At the time of acting, then, persons would have no idea which course of action would comply with defensive egoism. Nor, since their intentions to advance their interests would have at best a fortuitous connection with their welfare, would they have any grounds for cultivating self-interested dispositions. Striving not to be duped, they would thoroughly outwit themselves.

Impenetrable deceit bars adherence to consequentialist rules and permits persons to observe only those deontological rules with which compliance can be directly and immediately checked. For the same reasons that 'Guard your own interests' cannot serve as a code of conduct, other teleological prescriptions like 'Promote the general welfare' would also fail. Nor could dicta similar to 'Inflict no suffering' have a place in a code of conduct since torment can be disguised and faked. Only those deontological rules commending actions involving no other people, such as 'Blink five times after eating rice,' or instructing persons to affect easily distinguished individuals in indisputable ways, such as 'Spray fuchsia paint on joggers,' could constitute a tenable action guide if deceit and honesty were considered morally indifferent. Fast-acting methods of killing could be prohibited, but by hypothesis killing is

Foundations of Moral Interaction

permissible. Plainly, the prospects for conduct regulation under these conditions are superficial and negligible. Compliance with rules prescribing nonaggression would only be possible if persons engaged in so little activity that their subdued encounters could not spark injurious complications, and compliance with rules requiring mutual care would exceed the capabilities of agents unless these rules specified overt signs of successful care and disregarded the recipient's feelings.

Yet, supposing that persons could follow some narrow rules, there remains a difficulty about the constricted idea of personal responsibility necessitated by impenetrable deceit. A world riddled with undetectable deceit reduces what can be said about most human action to a parody of positivistic protocol sentences: "Here, now, ordered sequence of words, 'I am fine,' spoken by me," or "Here, now, run toward bus, executed by me." Characterizations of actions are confined to accounts of physical motions or lists of words uttered. In nearly all cases, neither the point of actions, the meaning strings of words convey, nor the rightness or wrongness of conduct can be discerned. This deracination calls into question the individual's ability to take responsibility for her own behavior. Though the expression signifying agency in my protocols, namely, 'by me,' is unproblematic given that these propositions are asserted as the behavior is occurring, the attribution of agency becomes problematic once the behavior is past.

Two considerations suggest that this temporal constraint would interfere with moral agency. First, moral agents must be competent to identify their behavior in retrospect because responsibility extends to consequences that may not appear until after the act is done. A person with a duty to spray joggers with fuchsia paint would do wrong if she negligently used defective paint that degenerated into a pea green hue soon after application. Second, moral agents must be able to recall their own conduct because aggrieved parties are rarely in a position to press accusations while infractions are being committed. If the spray-painter stayed at home watching television when she should have been out decorating joggers, weeks may pass before the joggers can find out that she had been assigned to paint-duty that day, and, as a result, their protesting her delinquency would be delayed. Thus, it is vital that persons be able to identify past as well as present conduct as their own if they are to count as responsible individuals.

Impenetrable deceit, we have seen, prevents persons from tracing the ramifications of their conduct. But persons must have good reasons for believing that alleged consequences of their acts really were caused by their conduct before they can take responsibility for them. A spray-painter who is accused of dereliction of duty but who cannot satisfy herself that her aerosol can has not been tampered with and who cannot ascertain whether or not a subsequent coating made the joggers green has no grounds for avowing responsibility for her intended beneficiaries' disappointment. If persons were to accept responsibility for epistemically opaque developments, their acknowledgments of responsibility, lacking any regular connection to actual events, would be empty formalities. Further, since persons would be intolerably vulnerable to frame-ups if they could be held accountable for unknown and unknowable consequences, they would be ill advised to assume responsibility for any alleged but unverifiable results.

The fallibility of memory adds another dimension to the problem of responsibility under the posited conditions. Whereas forgetfulness and the misunderstandings it perpetrates are normally nothing more than annoyances, the faultiness of memory would pose a formidable obstacle to responsibility if deceit were generally permissible. It is well known that distorted memories have no internal feature to set them apart from accurate ones. We rely on the coherence of our memories and the confirmation we occasionally get from others to assure us that our recollection of prior events correctly represents them. However, in a world of impenetrable deceit coherent and confirmed memories of past actions would not warrant a person's taking responsibility for them, even as discrete incidents separated from their consequences.

Once the prohibition on deceit has been dispensed with, a person may have both coherent and confirmed memories and yet be justified in doubting their accuracy. Her memories may be coherent because she has been following only one consistent acquaintance's feedback and ignoring the rest of her experience. But since that individual may be systematically inducing her to believe a pack of lies, the coherence of her memories does not provide evidence for their accuracy. Alternatively, a person might construct a unified explanation encompassing all of the events she has witnessed and reports she has received to produce a single cogent set of memories. Unfortunately, her inability to discover which of the items she has incorporated into her system of recollections are real vitiates any claim to accuracy that might be made on behalf of her memory. Worse still, a person cannot turn to anyone else for corroboration because she cannot know whether the testimony she obtains will be deceitful or honest. My spray-painter may know perfectly well that she neglected her duty this morning, but she may have genuine difficulty recalling what she did a week ago. In light of their inability to test the accuracy of their memories, persons in a world of impenetrable deceit would have only the slimmest basis either for acknowledging past behavior as their own or for repudiating past behavior attributed to them. The past would too quickly become moot.

Still the contention that a deceit-permissive gladiatorial moral system would prevent persons from functioning as moral agents might seem too extravagant since problems like the ones I have outlined arise in the world to which we are accustomed. People are not always able to discern all the ramifications of their conduct, their intentions are sometimes distorted when acted upon, and they do not command perfect recall of earlier actions. Despite these uncertainties, no one rushes to conclude that action is unclassifiable, that it makes no difference what a person's intentions are, or that personal responsibility is illusory.

Of course, it must be admitted that persons sometimes cannot penetrate experience in our familiar world. Nevertheless, there is a crucial difference between the world we live in and a world ordered according to gladiatorial morality: honesty is obligatory, and misunderstandings are usually corrigible in our world but not in the other. This is to say that, although an ingenious, far-reaching, deceptive scheme could be implemented in our accustomed social universe the chances of its ultimately succeeding and initiating a widespread syndrome of deceit are not good.

This state of affairs contrasts with my social chimera inasmuch as the prevalence of deception in the latter milieu coupled with principled indifference to it would protect individual acts of deception from being uncovered. Furthermore, whereas in our familiar world we are able to investigate any charge of deceit by collecting evidence which can be tested for trustworthiness, in my construct no one can ever be confident that the evidence she obtains is not itself delusory. No doubt, grandiose deceitful plots are sometimes brought off and never discovered in our world. But it is just because these are the exception rather than the rule or, in other words, because they impinge upon an otherwise coherent pattern of experience maintained by obligatory honesty that it is conceivable that we might isolate and unravel them.[15]

In the deceit-ridden world I have sketched, the ideas of moral choice and responsibility cancel out because they only have application in a world in which intentions are realized in intelligible action. But the experiential opacity of the world I have portrayed generally reduces intentions to decisions to move or refrain from moving in a particular way and accordingly reduces action to behavior. In this context, it is impossible to uphold any but the most rudimentary principles, and therefore distinguishing good and bad intentions and recognizing right and wrong conduct becomes an exercise in triviality. The idea of a moral choice, then, is unacceptably shrunken since moral choice under conditions of impenetrable deceit can take into consideration neither the complexity of human relations nor the exigencies of social existence.

Taking this line of thought a bit further, it becomes evident that the idea of responsibility must be eliminated, too, because it makes no sense to take responsibility for petty observances or for mere behavior. The concept of responsibility de-

Foundations of Moral Interaction

pends on our ability to know and control what we are doing, and it requires that persons be able to identify their actions well after they have finished doing them. But a world of impenetrable deceit would severely restrict autonomous action and preclude competent retrospective avowal of action. In sum, systemic deceit would prevent individuals from assuming the role of moral agents.

6. Two Types of Rescission by Design

A blanket issuance of inalienable liberties justifies a practice of defensive deceit. Thus, a member of a society that substitutes inalienable liberties for inalienable claim rights cannot assume that others are either forthright or devious and is left morally alone. The precariousness of the position occupied by these individuals will not allow them to refuse this defensive ploy, but the resulting impenetrable deceit obstructs personal planning as well as compliance with moral norms. Thus, any moral system countenancing this result is guaranteed to suffer from rescission by design. By sabotaging moral agency, such moral systems subvert their own implementation.

Yet, it might be countered that compliance with the obligation to engage in nondeceitful interpersonal relations when inalienable liberties are in force involves nothing more than a risk of death or injury. Since persons can be obligated to take risks with the objects of inalienable rights (only obligatory sacrifices of the objects of inalienable rights are ruled out), inalienable liberties could be instated without jeopardizing moral agency to the requisite degree. A moral system confining itself to imposing a risk of successful attacks on the objects of inalienable liberties, the objection concludes, could exact conformity to the obligation to engage in nondeceitful interpersonal relations and could not be accused of rescission by design.

This line of argument can best be answered by examining the plight of a person suddenly entering a society in which killing, coercion, torture, and severe deprivation are simply permissible. At the outset, she cannot reasonably assume that she is safe and cannot restrain herself until this assumption has been proven false. The consequences of misplaced optimism are too serious. A cautious approach—allowing otherwise impermissible dissembling and evasion, though not necessarily allowing preemptive strikes at others' interests—is warranted. What a person in this predicament eventually decides she may do to protect herself will depend on how grave she ascertains the risk of harm to herself to be. If she discovers that strict compliance with the prohibition on deceit invariably precipitates aggression with devastating consequences for herself, she is justified in using any defensive subterfuge. However, if she learns that she incurs only slightly more than the usual risk of harm by maintaining honest practices, she must consider whether the additional risk is worth taking. We are not, it must be remembered, always obligated to take a risk with the objects of our inalienable rights simply because it is only a risk.

The only plausible reason for acceding to an increased risk of being killed, enslaved, tormented, or deprived of basic necessities in a society that recognizes only liberties with respect to life, personal liberty, benign treatment, and satisfaction of basic needs is hope of gaining recognition for inalienable claim rights to these goods. If contests for the objects of these liberties are rare and predictable, this hope is not doomed, for these struggles have one of three possible origins. They may be inspired by popular misconceptions about provocation, they may represent vestiges of formerly defensible patterns of self-advancement, or they may anticipate forms of legitimate claim right infringement. Whichever is the case, conversion to a moral system incorporating inalienable claim rights should meet little resistance since the main difference between this moral system and one with these regimented liberties is that the former trades some archaic beliefs for substantially improved security. In light of the fact that the conventions of this society require abstention from indiscriminate exercise of

Foundations of Moral Interaction

the full range of permissions inalienable liberties may grant, a stranger's conformity to ordinary moral principles is minimally risky and arguably not supererogatory.

In contrast, the prognosis is poor for a society in which aggression is frequent and erratic. Improvisational violence brings with it fearsome vulnerability and desperate defensive maneuvering, that is, gladiatorial morality with impenetrable deceit. In this hostile environment, an individual cannot be confident that her moral example will persuade her hosts to acknowledge inalienable claim rights. Nor can she be sanguine about her chances of survival if she clings to honesty and restraint. Under these circumstances, it would be supererogatory, if not fatuous, for a person to endanger herself.

In regard to their regulation of conduct concerning life, liberty, benign treatment, and satisfaction of basic needs, moral systems can be located on a gradated spectrum. At one pole is recognition of unrestricted inalienable liberties. At the other is recognition of inalienable claim rights. In between lie incremental restraints on aggression. Moral systems close to the maximal liberty pole tend to collapse into that stand since they offer no incentive for observing their minor restraining maxims. Similarly, moral systems near the claim rights end of the array become virtually indistinguishable from their prototype since only subtle differences over the permissibility of violence separate them. Indeed, which moral system belongs at this pole is a matter of controversy since people disagree about which rights abridgments are justifiable. Though it may not be possible to specify precisely where on this spectrum of permissions personal insecurity justifiably defeats moral scruples, it is plain that moral systems spread out along the spectrum are volatile: if their brutality does not incline them to degenerate under pressure into deadly license, their approximation to humaneness encourages reforms solidifying personal protections.

Moral systems containing inalienable liberties with respect to life, personal liberty, benign treatment, and satisfaction of basic needs have the defect of rescission by design. Either they foster sensibilities which make them prone to transformation into moral systems recognizing inalienable claim rights, or they promote treachery and suspicions which, if left unchecked, ultimately prevent any moral principles from being followed. The former kind of moral system is benignly self-rescinding; the latter is invidiously self-rescinding.[16] Neither, finally, is satisfactory. It follows that there cannot be inalienable liberties if interaction conforming to a satisfactry moral system is to be possible. Invidious liberties create a social environment inimical to all moral relations, while benign liberties must be alienated to establish social recognition for inalienable claim rights. Though the criteria I defended in chapter 2—inalienable rights have objects that are necessary for moral agency, and they have objects that cannot be sacrificed obligatorily—do not rule out inalienable liberties, the fundamental structure of moral interaction does. Accordingly, the rights to life, personal liberty, benign treatment, and satisfaction of basic needs can no more be renounced by fiat than they can be renounced conscientiously. These rights are inalienable.

5

Possession of Inalienable Rights

Human rights, it is often said, are rights all persons have simply by virtue of being human. However, as we have seen, persons have inalienable rights because adequate moral systems must be neither self-defeating nor self-rescinding or, in other words, because adequate moral systems must sustain moral agency. Although there may not be any moral agents who are not humans (exploration of outer space will tell), there certainly are humans who are not yet moral agents and some who have little or no prospect of attaining this status. Thus, mere humanity does not suffice for possession of inalienable rights, and humanity may not prove necessary for possession of them, either. Furthermore, since moral agency is not a single uniform property—different persons exhibit it in different ways—it is possible that the content or moral force of inalienable rights varies collaterally. These reflections raise four central questions regarding possession of inalienable rights:

1. Is this divergence from the tradition that to be human is to have inalienable rights warranted?

2. Does this concentration on moral agency as a qualification for inalienable rights possession render them inegalitarian?
3. Are inalienable rights insensible of the needs and interests of children and morally incompetent adults?
4. Can any protections for animals be derived from inalienable rights doctrine?

To answer these queries is to dispose of doubts about excessive elitism as well as overextended populism within the theory of inalienable rights and to clarify the sense in which inalienable rights comprise an egalitarian position.

1. Species Membership and the Qualifications for Inalienable Rights

Salubrious as the conjunction of basic rights with universality in the domain of the human has been from a practical standpoint, the implication that individuals possess certain rights because they are members of a select species sanctifies a conceptual muddle. Individuals qualify for rights as individuals, not as members of species. It may be the case that all or nearly all of the members of a species have a certain right. But if so, they have this right because of properties that characterize all or most members of the species. In view of the impracticality of ascertaining which individuals meet the criteria for various rights on a case by case basis, it may be advisable to presume that all members of a species have a certain right. Yet, this pragmatic approximation should not seduce us into viewing rights possession as a function of species membership. For the biological definitions of species are too sparse to provide the information needed to establish conclusions about rights possession.

That membership in a species is not by itself relevant to possession of rights becomes clear once attention is diverted from members of the human species and focused on some other species, like gophers and robins, to which we are less emotionally attached. Let us grant for the sake of argument that most gophers have a right to a burrow because digging a burrow is the normal gopher's natural way of providing itself with shelter. Along the same lines, suppose that robins have a right to a nest. Is membership in these species the basis for this attribution of rights? The fatuity of attributing a right to a burrow to a mutant gopher who instinctively climbs a tree and constructs a nest of twigs and leaves reveals that species membership is not the critical factor. If anything, this sport should have a right to a nest despite the fact that it is a gopher. Evidently, the properties that usually characterize gophers, not gopherhood, would constitute the basis of our attribution of rights to gophers.

Whatever our ingrained suppositions about the bearing of biological taxonomy on possession of inalienable rights, it becomes plain on reflection that limiting the protection afforded by inalienable rights to whichever capabilities constitute common denominators for the human species would hardly be desirable. Attributes shared by every human being are apt to characterize most living things or, at any rate, most mammals. Few properties characterize every human being (infants as well as adults, ailing as well as healthy individuals), and those that do turn out to be so basic that they extend to similar forms of life as well. All humans breathe, register signs of neural activity, and need nourishment, but all goldfish do, too. As a result, reliance on capabilities that characterize all human beings as qualifications for inalienable rights severely limits the kinds of goods that can be objects of these rights and precipitously diminishes their impact on moral deliberation.

Supposing for the moment that the abilities to respire, fire neurons, and hunger for nourishment qualify individuals for inalienable rights, it must be asked what rights these individuals might have. Presumably, there must be a rational relationship between the qualifications for a right and possession of it. The need for nourishment could conceivably qualify an individual for a right to suitable comestibles, perhaps to intravenously administered nutriments on occasion, but not for a right to the pursuit of happiness unless the need for nourishment signals a desire for well-being in the broad sense. If an individual cannot enjoy and will forever be unable to enjoy the good conferred by a right, attributing it to him is otiose. Thus, the capabilities of prospective right-holders restrict the content of the rights they may possess, and qualifications for inalienable rights geared to universal human possession of these rights would rule out the right to personal liberty, the right to an education, and all other rights which presuppose right-holders' mobility or intelligence.

Natural rights for which all humans would qualify would entitle right-holders only to the most rudimentary benefits. However, two accounts of the right to life illustrate a more serious problem, that is, the weakening of the protection these rights would bestow on each human. Locke holds that the capacity for rationality and vulnerability are necessary and together sufficient conditions for possession of the right to life.[1] Alternatively, the capacity to register signs of neural activity and mortality could be considered necessary and together sufficient conditions for possession of this right. Compare the role of these two rights in the deliberations of a person who must decide whether to kill an average goldfish or an innocent, normally endowed, adult human being. Locke's version is dispositive, whereas my improvisation leaves the issue unresolved. Admittedly, Locke's account decides matters on the wrong grounds, but, at least, he does not pretend that this choice embroils the chooser in a vexing moral quandary pitting irreconcilable rights against each other.

Consistency obliges us both to limit the protection of rights to those creatures that qualify for them and also to extend this protection to all such creatures. If capabilities common to the human species are sufficient conditions for possession of inalienable rights, these rights must not be used to provide extra security for human capabilities which other right-holders lack, and nonhumans that share these elemental capabilities must fully enjoy their rights. On the face of it, acknowledging natural rights which all humans along with sundry fauna are guaranteed to possess elevates moral drivel to the status of serious moral dilemma. But why should this shift be regarded as generating misguided ethical consternation rather than as revealing genuine moral difficulty where none had been noticed?

The trouble with founding the right to life and other inalienable rights on capabilities common to all the members of the human species is that they will not turn out to be capabilities that anyone has compelling reasons to protect. The ability to register signs of neural activity, for example, may seem consequential in the context of recent euthanasia cases, but this is because this ability is taken as a sign of other potentialities that members of the human species typically have. The triviality of this capacity taken by itself becomes evident once it is noticed that persons share it with goldfish and a host of other creatures. No doubt there is a good deal to be said on behalf of nonhuman animals, but their virtues are quite distinct from any attributes they happen to share with humans. Indeed, what worse sort of speciesism could there be than the attitude that members of other species can only gain rights insofar as they resemble humans?

The upshot of these ruminations on people, goldfish, and rights is that the capacity to benefit from a right does not adequately explain the grounds for possession of it. This is obvious in the case of rights that are generated by transactions. If a person agrees to pay another person $10 for ten bales of hay, the seller gains a right to $10 from the buyer. The seller's neighbor who desperately needs $10 but who has no role in this bargain cannot gain a right to the buyer's payment by virtue of the fact that she would benefit from having the money, whereas the seller is too rich to notice $10 one way or the other. Since the neighbor is not a party to the agreement, she has no claim on the buyer's money unless she can establish such a claim on independent grounds.

Yet, when attention is turned to moral rights that are not created by transactions, it is understandable that the capacity to benefit from these rights would be thought a sufficient condition for possession of them.[2] Accounting for possession of these rights presents obstacles that sometimes look insuperable, and invoking capacities to benefit neatly ties the content of rights to the individuals who possess them. Nevertheless, the capacity to benefit from the protection afforded by such rights is only a threshold issue. Inanimate, mechanical, insensate, and self-sufficient entities could not have rights to life, personal liberty, benign treatment, and satisfaction of basic needs since it would be logically impossible to respect or violate their rights. But being alive, locomotive, sentient, and dependent on the natural environment for the means of survival does not suffice for possession of inalienable rights. If it did, these rights would be equivalent to undifferentiated duties not to kill, coerce, torment, or deprive any individual capable of suffering these types of maltreatment. In that case, the rights to life, liberty, benign treatment, and satisfaction of basic needs would have no supervenient moral force.

The proposition that a particular individual has, for example, a right to life is not just a sonorous way of saying that *ceteris paribus* it would be good if he were allowed to go on living. Attributing a right to life to someone entitles him to demand that he not be disturbed in the enjoyment of his life and secures him in the knowledge that only incontrovertible, rarely apposite reasons could justify anyone else's killing him against his will. In the case of moral dependents—individuals unable to assert their own rights—competent individuals must assume responsibility for assuring their wards' enjoyment of their rights. Thus, if children have rights, benevolent adults must protect them from wicked adults and must also supervise them in order to protect them from one another. Unless these services were provided for the morally helpless, their rights would be reduced to the adult population's duties of respect since rights assertion is not possible for them and rights respect is not possible among them. Accordingly, attributing rights to life, personal liberty, benign treatment, and satisfaction of basic needs to every creature that might enjoy these rights would commit adult humans to such tasks as policing carnivores and supplying them with alternate means of sustenance. Apart from the zoological questionability of this intervention in nature, the project of paternal enforcement of these presumptive natural rights has unacceptable moral consequences.

In the attempt to secure special moral protection for all vulnerabilities, none would be secured. If more individuals have claims to noninterference and aid than can possibly be respected and all of these claims are equally weighty, a lottery is the only solution. In extreme situations, this procedure may be a welcome last resort. But if due to an unmanageable claim load these lotteries were to become commonplace events, rights would be drained of any moral force beyond impartiality. Rights protect vulnerabilities and in so doing benefit right-holders, but vulnerabilities are too widespread to shield routinely with rights. So as not to confound moral judgment, rights possession must be confined to a set of individuals whose claims can ordinarily be honored.

Inalienable rights pose a further obstacle to a benefit-based analysis of rights possession. The capacity to benefit from these rights could not fully account for possession of them unless this capacity explained why right-holders could not renounce them. But since a capacity to benefit from a right does not entail an inability to forgo this benefit, possession of inalienable rights must depend on some additional factor.

The capacity inalienable rights single out for protection supplies a reason over and above compassion for recognizing them. Inalienable rights are rights that moral systems must recognize in order not to be self-defeating and self-rescinding. They are rights that individuals need in order to conduct themselves morally and that secure goods that can only be supererogatorily sacrificed for others' benefit. Along with protecting right-holders from untimely death and unnecessary misery, inalienable rights enable individuals to engage in moral interaction. Since this enabling function distinguishes inalienable rights from other moral rights, inalienable right-holders must be capable of moral agency. Furthermore, the requirement that goods secured by inalienable rights be immune to obligatory sacrifice would be unintelligible unless paradigmatic inalienable right-holders had this capacity. Only moral agents can incur obligations and make supererogatory gestures. Though many individuals lacking the capacity for moral agency are capable of enjoying the incidental protections inalienable rights afford because they are vulnerable to the same harms to which individuals with the capacity for moral agency are subject, only individuals capable of enjoying the guarantees of inalienable rights for the reason moral systems must grant them are inalienable right-holders.

2. The Equality of Inalienable Rights

That inalienable rights must be equal rights, that is, rights that entitle every right-holder to accomplish the same things in the same range of circumstances, is often accepted more or less as an article of faith.[3] But this egalitarianism could be challenged on two grounds. First, since capacities for moral agency vary, it might be urged that inalienable rights should be distributed accordingly. Second, since there are good and bad moral agents, it might be argued that their inalienable rights should reflect their moral merit. Neither of these lines of objection successfully makes the case for elitism, however, because they both overlook the foundational role of inalienable rights with respect to moral agency.

The capacity for moral agency is not an irreducible ability to see what would be right and to do it. Apprehending the right course of action and carrying it through summon a whole panoply of capabilities, and different individuals, each of whom is capable of moral agency, have distinctive configurations of constitutive strengths and weaknesses. To justify his position, an advocate of unequal inalienable rights might advert to these variations in endowment, insisting that some of these complex capacities are better than others.

It is important to notice, however, that the value of a person's idiosyncratic combination of capabilities depends on historical conditions and on the unfolding of his own biography. While physical endurance, intellectual perspicacity, emotional stamina, and subtle sensibility generally contribute to moral agency, there is no single ideal endowment, nor is there any way to assign different endowments to fixed positions on a scale of preferability. Under some circumstances maximal physical endurance or emotional stamina would be preferable to a high degree of development in other faculties. In fact, it is easy to imagine situations in which great intellectual powers or acute sensibility would be handicaps. But there are also circumstances in which physical endurance or emotional stamina would be of minor importance or could prove to be liabilities. Thus, any particular mix of strengths and weaknesses will be appraised as more or less desirable depending on circumstances.

To link the moral force of inalienable rights to these shifts in the value of an individual's distinctive endowment would be to weaken severely the protection afforded by these rights. Suppose that persons have rights weighted according to the adaptation of each right-holder's personality to cope with the circumstances she confronts. Anyone bent on attacking someone else could first manipulate these circumstances so as to reduce the stringency of her chosen enemy's rights, thereby removing the moral obstacles to her plan. Though right-holders might try to resist these machinations, their rights would not bar them. Inalienable rights cannot shelter right-holders from devastating, uncontrollable fortune; still, if they are to protect right-holders at all, they cannot be buffeted about by insidious designs.

Paradoxically, humanity must be viewed in the aggregate for inalienable rights to function on behalf of the individual. Having a capacity for moral agency enables a person to interact morally and allows others to rely on his self-control. Under circumstances tolerably conducive to moral interaction, that is, circumstances in which inalienable rights can be respected, exceptional abilities are insignificant in maintaining moral responsibility. They may sharpen moral perspicacity or stiffen moral resolve. But unless persons assume special posts, their extraordinary abilities do not burden them with more moral responsibility than others are expected to bear. Diverse capacities for moral agency, then, do not warrant unequal inalienable rights.

Still, an intransigent elitist can turn from capacities to results. Whatever their innate capabilities, some moral agents turn out to be good while others turn out to be bad. Persons could begin life with maximally stringent inalienable rights and keep these powerful rights long enough to prove their mettle. As the bad and the imperfect revealed themselves, they could be demoted to less stringent inalienable rights. Ultimately, only the supremely good and the innocent young would enjoy the full protection of these rights. Of course, the assumptions that persons do sort themselves into good and bad categories and that their moral deserts can be accurately appraised are highly dubious. Nevertheless, it is critical to see why granting these assumptions would not justify introduction of graduated inalienable rights.

Substantial differences in the moral force of inalienable rights would permit abridgment in different ranges of circumstances. These rights devaluations would ostensibly be predicated on right-holders' reduced qualifications for these rights. Since bad agents act immorally more often than good ones, the argument goes, their capacity for moral agency must be impaired. Consequently, they are less qualified for inalienable rights and do not deserve the full protection of these rights.

Two difficulties immediately tell against this position. First, individuals must meet two qualifications for inalienable rights. Not only must they be capable of moral agency, but they must also be vulnerable to the types of harm which inalienable rights forbid. Evil persons are no less susceptible to being killed, coerced, tormented, and deprived of basic necessities than virtuous persons are. From the standpoint of this vulnerability qualification, then, these kinds of individuals are equally qualified for inalienable rights. Second, being a moral agent should not be conflated with being a virtuous agent. The former characterization informs us that the individual can be held responsible for his conduct; the latter indicates that his conduct is usually praiseworthy. A moral monster may be as responsible for his outrages as a minor transgressor is. Accordingly, the capacity for moral agency, not an admirable character, is the prerequisite for possession of inalienable rights.

Self-defeating and self-rescinding moral systems are unacceptable because they are capable of terminating moral interaction by preventing persons from acting as responsible agents. Adequate moral systems recognize inalienable rights and thereby ensure the basic conditions of autonomy. In sum, these rights secure the moral environment which constitutes the opportunity for persons to be virtuous (or, for that matter, vicious). For this reason, prorating a person's inalienable rights in accordance with diminishing moral merit becomes a self-fulfilling prophecy. Persons who have done badly are encouraged to persist or do worse by the decreased security devaluation of their rights brings. To the extent that acting honorably would interfere with their ability to make up for the inferiority of their rights, these persons might understandably opt for dishonor. After all, their needs are the same as others'.

Weakening the stringency of persons' inalienable rights to match their poor moral performance ignores the needs that partially qualify them for these rights, mistakes the moral agency qualification for a virtue requirement, and tricks the right-holder into further depredations. Only equal inalienable rights mirror the equality of right-holders' qualifications for these rights and ensure that right-holders can be held equally responsible for their conduct.[4] Though inalienable rights cannot prevent the advent of pervasive *in extremis* scarcity or personal tragedy from disrupting this balance of mutual responsibility, equal inalienable rights maintain this equilibrium insofar as morality can.

A graduated schedule of inalienable rights would establish a social order in which some individuals could be treated as persons stigmatized by lower castes have been treated. In the normal course of events, persons ascribed weaker rights could be used by their betters, and, in a catastrophe, these unfortunates would almost certainly be sacrificed before anyone possessing rights ranked higher on the stringency scale. To justify this inequality, we must be convinced that some individuals are capable of moral agency but do not qualify for inalienable rights because, not requiring life, personal liberty, benign treatment, and satisfaction of basic needs to conduct themselves morally, they may be obligated to sacrifice these goods altruistically. In other words, it must be shown that there are moral agents who do not have the four inalienable rights. Because their rights to life, personal liberty, benign treatment, and satisfaction of basic needs could be forfeited or revoked, these individuals could licitly be deprived of part or all of the protection of these rights.

Curiously, not the wicked but the extraordinarily good are most likely to be able to disregard their own most urgent interests in the service of lofty moral principles. Cowards and voluptuaries crumble at the slightest menace or temptation while heroes and saints withstand prodigious threats and enticements. These discrepancies in moral fortitude suggest that equal inalienable rights could prove patently inutile in a crisis involving conflicting rights since they might protect a courageous right-holder who could have endured the hardship while abandoning an ignoble right-holder to founder. To avoid this misallocation of moral resources, it might be urged, the virtuous should be awarded less stringent inalienable rights.

This argument for unequal inalienable rights attends insufficiently to the moral obstacles in the way of detecting superior moral strength and to the singular advantages of the right as a moral instrument. Plainly, character and strength of will are not observable properties, and moral excellence and scurrility are found in all kinds of people. Accordingly, nothing short of a licensing system would enable decision-makers to identify persons with less stringent rights. Such a certification program would involve testing for moral virtue by thrusting candidates into situations contrived to expose their moral strengths or deficiencies. To sort out the population, it would ultimately be necessary to ascertain how each individual would react in the face of moral horror. But to make this determination, it would be necessary to present agents with calamities in which their moral performance could be observed. This enterprise is morally out of the question. It is clearly wrong to precipitate catastrophe, and, even if catastrophes could be convincingly faked, it would remain wrong to subject every person to these horrifying conditions periodically in order to check on moral progress or backsliding. Since there is no morally acceptable way to license moral agents, differentially stringent inalienable rights are impracticable.

More important still, unlike duties of self-preservation which lock agents into giving themselves preference, inalienable rights allow individuals to prefer others. Whereas an exceptionally noble and generous person who is duty-bound to protect his own interests must be convinced that countervailing considerations supersede this duty before he can justifiably come to the aid of his weaker fellows, a similarly disposed rightholder can adopt a self-sacrificial course of action purely out of sympathy for others and regardless of whether it will procure a greater amount of good.[5] Equal inalienable rights do not secure superfluous benefits for extraordinarily virtuous individuals at the expense of ordinary people. Just the contrary, these rights make extraordinary virtue possible while acknowledging the limitations most agents labor under. As a result, it is unnecessary to take draconian steps to identify the morally good, for rights enable them to reveal themselves in the event.

3. The Dispossessed

Any acceptable moral system must confer equal inalienable rights on all individuals who are capable of moral agency. Because abridgment of these rights can never be morally required, though it is sometimes permissible, and because alienable rights do not bar obligatory infliction of comparable misfortunes on their bearers, inalienable right-holders enjoy a moral edge over other individuals. This is not to say that inalienable right-holders are always to be preferred to others but rather that when inalienable rights are at stake, the presumption is that these right-holders' claims take precedence.

The strict criterion for possession of inalienable rights coupled with the moral advantage inalienable right-holders enjoy may seem out of phase with our everyday convictions about our moral relations to those who fail to qualify. In particular, nonhuman animals, children, and morally incompetent humans are not capable of moral agency but cannot be mistreated with moral impunity. We are not free to starve our pets wantonly, to beat our children brutally, or to use incompetent humans for experimental purposes. Yet, none of these kinds of individual seems to be entitled to the protection of inalienable rights.

While it is clear that moral agents may have duties to treat other kinds of individuals humanely though these individuals have no rights to this consideration, the exclusion of nonhuman animals, incompetent humans, and, especially, normal children from the class of inalienable right-holders remains somewhat unpalatable. Our qualms about nonhuman animals are a fitting sympathetic response to publicized abuse of these creatures by scientific investigators and agribusiness. Nevertheless, I shall argue, there is no basis for granting any inalienable right to animals. In contrast, a convincing case can be made for acknowledging a derivative, but inalienable right, held by children.

4. Children

Neither animals nor children are capable of moral agency (we do not hold members of these groups morally responsible). Unlike animals, however, normal children have the potential to become moral agents (this is why we teach them to act responsibly). Children are not able to engage in reciprocal moral interaction, but eventually most of them will be able to do so, provided that their development is not stunted. In order for a child's moral development to proceed apace, she must be treated as if she qualified for the rights to life and satisfaction of basic needs; pain must be administered judiciously and in the service of moral training; and such enforced restraints as are forbidden by the right to personal liberty must be progressively removed as her judgment matures. This care can be summed up as a right to moral education.

The right to moral education should not be collapsed into the right to an education which often appears on lists of human rights. Yet, these rights are closely related. It is necessary to teach a child the language that is spoken in her community, to give her guidance and practice in deliberating about conduct, and in many communities to teach her elementary literary and mathematical skills in order to prepare her to assume the role of a responsible agent. The right to moral education entails a right to training in certain linguistic and reasoning skills; however, it does not entail a right to be familiarized with a humanistic or scientific heritage. The right to an education is both broader and narrower than the right to moral education. The right to moral education incorporates the treatment children ought to be accorded in regard to the four primary inalienable rights, as well as explicitly pedagogical care. But the right to an education entitles persons to more extensive cultural exposure than the right to moral education requires.

I shall take it for granted that no one denies that parents ought to provide their offspring with the minimal nurture sketched above. But questions linger as to whether all adult human beings are obligated to secure a moral education for all children and whether the source of this obligation is an inalienable right possessed by every child. These questions are best understood as opposite sides of the question of whether the criteria of adequacy that imply inalienable rights for adults also imply inalienable rights for children.

Infants are oblivious to morality; very young children comply with moral principles only because they are told to do so; older children take morality into account only erratically. Yet, despite the fact that these classes of individuals uphold moral systems, at best, serendipitously, only a stunningly myopic view of moral intercourse could fail to see that a moral system countenancing obligations to withhold moral education from normal children would be self-defeating. Though this kind of moral system might slowly grind moral interaction to a standstill rather than bringing it to a precipitous halt, its capacity to suppress moral potential is indistinguishable in ultimate effect from a capacity to order destruction of moral agents. Either way the moral system can enjoin termination of moral interaction.

Likewise, the requirement that adequate moral systems not be self-defeating entails that adults capable of giving birth to normal babies cannot be obligated to refrain from procreating and that women who have conceived normal fetuses cannot be obligated to abort them. However, since moral systems need not be self-perpetuating, it is not incumbent upon them to prescribe the propagation of the species. Accordingly, neither potential fetuses nor potential infants have inalienable rights; there is no inalienable right to be conceived or to be brought to term. Rather, the requirement that moral systems not be self-defeating protects the freedom of prospective parents. Unless their reproductive capacities are so severely impaired that their offspring are bound to be morally ineducable or a fetus they conceive proves too severely compromised to be morally educable, they cannot be obligated not to procreate. Indeed, these misfortunes would not automatically obligate them not to procreate.

Still, it might be objected that an inalienable right to moral education for children is unnecessary. Since parents usually love their children and eagerly care for them, there is no need to encumber others with responsibility for strangers' offspring. And failing parental instincts, the requirement that moral systems not be self-defeating could be met by an injunction to rear that fraction of the baby population sufficient to carry on moral relations.

Callous though this proposal undeniably is, it is not immediately evident why adequate moral systems must reject it. Admittedly, a moral system would be self-defeating if it could prohibit giving moral education to individuals who are capable of learning, but the proposed program for rearing strategic numbers of these individuals relies on a permission to withhold moral education, not an obligation to do so. The contention is merely that there is nothing wrong with excluding some children from the moral community and hence that they have no inalienable right to moral education.

The question of whether children have an inalienable right to moral education must be separated from other questions about how they should be treated. Killing a child destroys a living creature as well as a moral potential; banishing or simply ignoring a child subjects a sentient creature to pain and privation; and enslaving a child warps a creature's development. Since moral considerations independent of inalienable rights undoubtedly militate against such practices, a pure case of moral agency excision must be devised. Robert Nozick's "experience machine" admirably serves this purpose.[6] The experience machine consists of a tank with electrodes programmed to stimulate the subject's brain so as to give her experiences like the ones usually produced by living. Children not elected for moral education could be consigned to these tanks where they would undergo a sequence of engrossing and blissful experiences. This arrangement would neither decrease the world's life total nor increase its sum of misery or perversion, but it would prevent moral agents from maturing. Assuming that enough children were morally educated to keep moral interaction flourishing, why could adequate moral systems not permit a tank program?

An initial objection to tank life, one anticipated by Nozick, is that the child would not actually do the things she experienced doing. She might be given the experience of writing a great novel and believe herself to have written one, but there would be no book to show for it. She would leave no mark on the world. To remedy this problem, Nozick invents the "result machine," which "produces in the world any result you would produce and injects your vector input into any joint activity."⁷ It would produce a book corresponding to the experience of writing it.

Still, the result machine's supplementary effects only partially dispel the tank dweller's misapprehension of her existence. When a person has the experience of writing a book, she believes both that a book is being written and also that she is writing it. Likewise, when a person experiences friendship, she believes herself to be participating in a relationship with another person. But, in reality, the result machine would be supplying the book or friend and also carrying out the appropriate actions for the tank dweller. Thus, a tank dweller would believe herself to be a functioning member of society, although the machines would have usurped her capacity to do anything. A person who places a baby in the custody of the tank must choose between condemning the child to a lifelong experience of unrelieved passivity and isolation or to unabated delusion regarding her activities and interaction with others. Since subjecting a child to a life devoid of initiative and fellowship deprives her of much more than moral agency, let us grant that tank programmers would be obliged to include various projects and interpersonal contacts in their charges' programs. Though all of these experiences would be incorrigible delusions, tank dwellers would be saved from the dismal prospect of incessant vacuity.

Notice, now, that the tank dweller would not be the only individual deluded by the machines' operations. The person the tank dweller's result machine befriends, for example, must also believe she is involved in a real friendship. If the real-world friend did not believe this, the result machine could be accused of faking the results. Just as the result machine cannot substitute a sheaf of rave reviews for a great novel, it cannot hire an actor to mimic friendship instead of making a friend for the tank dweller. Thus, persons outside the tanks would undergo real-world experiences intermingled with phantom experiences induced by result machines, and they would be unable to distinguish these two types of experience.

The result machine's ingenious mediation of this interpenetration between the tanks and the world obliges moral agents to treat tank dwellers as if they, too, were moral agents. Vulnerability to murder, subjugation, torment, and deprivation along with a realized capacity for moral agency qualifies individuals for inalienable rights. But in simulating these characteristics in their projections on behalf of their wards, result machines would engender pseudo-inalienable rights for tank dwellers, and they would impose pseudo-obligations to respect these rights on moral agents. Admittedly, the tank dwellers' result machine projections, not the tank dwellers themselves, would be the beneficiaries of this treatment.[8] Nevertheless, from the standpoint of the moral agents who are responding to these figments, the important point is that, contrary to their intent, tanking children relieves them of no moral burdens. Since they cannot discern the difference between a person with an inalienable right and a tank manifestation with a pseudo-right, they must respect all of these claims indiscriminately to avoid violating genuine rights.

Still, an advocate of tanking unwanted and unneeded children could concede that tank dwellers would indirectly elicit moral responses but could insist that this one-sided attentiveness is tolerable provided that the guardian-child stage, and with it the especially onerous duty of moral education, were stricken from the tank repertory. One obstacle to this editing of the experiences available to tank dwellers is that experience machines may not be able to condense moral education, let alone catapult infants immediately into adult experience. Surely, some preparation would be necessary before these machines could impart to tank dwellers such sophisticated experiences as understanding witty conversation and being gratified at the delicacy of a courteous gesture. However, even if we grant experience machines the power to dispense with the experience of growing up, the tank program remains an unacceptable population management scheme.

Whether result machines engage independent moral agents in nurturing the projections of their charges or only in mature interaction with these projections, a moral system permitting tank life compels moral agents to accord tank dwellers the same moral consideration that they owe right-holders. Under normal conditions, this obscuring of the line between moral agency and inveterate moral incompetence would merely lead moral agents to display more concern for some individuals than they deserve. Though foolish in the abstract, this excessive solicitude would usually be harmless, rather like eccentrically intense devotion to a pet. However, in a grave crisis necessitating the sacrifice of some individuals, the consequences of the machines' fabrications could well be dire. Specifically, the claims of result machine projections, having the same apparent force as those of normal children and adults, might be honored instead of those of real inalienable right-holders. In the wake of this debacle, experience machines might proceed through their programs, but no one would remain outside the tanks from whom result machines could elicit a moral response.

Moral systems that permit adults to eschew responsibility for raising children by placing them in tanks have the defect of rescission by design. To permit suppression of moral potential is to authorize creation of an opaque social network which bars moral agents from identifying real claimants and which consequently sabotages rational moral deliberation and responsible conduct. If persons cannot penetrate the result machines' illusions, they cannot separate duties of respect contingent upon genuine rights from ersatz duties. This moral blindness obliges them to squander attention on phantoms and prevents them from making informed choices when apparent rights conflict. Inasmuch as these individuals act in ignorance of the moral import of their conduct, they cannot be held responsible for their misjudgments and cannot be regarded as full moral agents in interpersonal matters. Suppression of some children's moral potential, then, infects the whole moral community, and moral systems that authorize this practice jeopardize moral interaction.

Still, there is an obvious rejoinder to the argument I have presented: whereas the experience and result machines are counterfactual, the problem before us concerns the morality of conduct in the known or probable world. As things are, the only way to suppress a child's moral potential, apart from killing her, is to handicap her so severely that her impediments are readily apparent. Realistically, withholding moral education from some children would not obfuscate social relations so as to hamper moral agents' knowledgeable deliberation and conduct.

While it must be admitted that ordinarily the suppression of a child's moral potential is empirically discoverable (albeit her potential for recovery may be in doubt), it does not follow that there is no right to moral education, for it remains to consider the perspective of the right-holder, namely, the child. Inalienable rights, I have contended, cannot be renounced because they entitle right-holders to goods which it is always supererogatory to sacrifice altruistically. But children, since they cannot comprehend the consequences of refusing moral education, are in a position neither to sacrifice this good, whether supererogatorily or obligatorily, nor to renounce their right to it. To cope with this asymmetry, an equivalent of rights renunciation and supererogation must be found. For a child, the only way to lose a right is to have it revoked. Accordingly, the right to moral education is inalienable if it cannot be revoked because it can never be obligatory for an adult to deprive a child of the object of the right. Though it can be permissible to abridge any inalienable right, it can only be obligatory to abridge an alienable right.

To abridge the right to moral education without the mitigating assistance of Nozick's machines is to brutalize a child in the strictest sense of the term. It is both to treat the child brutally and to make her a brute. Because children are helpless and their wounds leave them physically and emotionally scarred, abusing them is unspeakable, the lowest sort of criminality. This extra opprobrium that we reserve for child abuse suggests that no predicament could convert comparable actions into obligations. Surely, if killing, subjugating, torturing, and depriving adults of basic necessities cannot be obligatory, there is no reason to suppose that subjecting children to similarly cruel treatment could be. At most, the bleakest circumstances can render such conduct permissible.

The potential for moral agency is integral to the normal human child. To suppress it, the child must be severely incapacitated and frustrated, if not destroyed. Moreover, the experience and result machines show that, if a child whose moral potential is extinguished could be allowed so much as a simulacrum of normal development and contact with the world, she would extract full moral consideration from others. So inextricable from the child is her moral potential that it is not possible to see normal childish behavior stripped of this dimension, and so firm are our precepts requiring that children be accorded gentle care that they are never nullified. Though it is hoped that parents will raise their own children and that parental affection will obviate assertion of the right to moral education, it is clear that moral education is not the exclusive province of willing parents or a calculating moral community. It is an inalienable right held by every normal child which any adequate moral system must recognize.

5. Animals

A moral community requires continuity over generations of moral agents. It will disintegrate despite the presence of the original members if provisions are not made for the moral education of new members. Thus, a moral system that fails to recognize an inalienable right to moral education is unacceptable. Can the same be said for a moral system that does not grant animals a suitably adjusted inalienable right to care?[9]

The most promising support for such a right stems from the fact that animals occupy ecological niches. If the natural environment inhabited by moral agents is destroyed, they will be destroyed, too. Consequently, it might be urged that moral systems must confer rights to be nurtured and protected on animals in order to ensure the survival of moral agents. One difficulty in this proposal is, of course, that it entails inalienable rights for every entity that has an ecological function—panda bears, mosquitoes, and ferns alike. As noted above, neither individuals nor states could keep track of this vast system of inalienable rights and this burgeoning population of rightholders. Since these rights could only be respected haphazardly, they would trivialize other rights without improving the survival outlook for the creatures said to possess them.

Still, it could be urged that rights to noninterference are easy to respect and would suffice for animals. Animals need no special cultivation to fulfill their ecological roles; they need only be left alone. Appealing as this vision of the world as a wildlife sanctuary may in some respects be, its direct and rigid opposition to industry and recreation, that is, to human liberty, seems exceedingly retrograde. Yet, it must be asked whether an argument paralleling the one for the right to moral education can be made on behalf of animals. For if such an argument can be sustained, the implications for the course of civilization would be momentous.

The defense of an inalienable right to moral education for children proceeded in two main steps. First, it was shown that an obligation to suppress moral potential could prove incompatible with the persistence of moral interaction and, therefore, that a moral system capable of generating such an obligation would be self-defeating. Second, it was shown that a permission to suppress moral potential provided only that the population of the moral community did not sink to a dangerously low level would subject those deprived of moral education to empty or deluded lives and, furthermore, that this practice would prevent otherwise competent moral agents from obtaining information crucial to their deliberations about their conduct. Thus, a moral system issuing this permission would also be flawed by rescission by design.

Though there is overwhelming evidence that civilization has often advanced with woeful indifference to nature and that continuing this destruction unabated could eventually make the earth uninhabitable, it remains undeniable that some kinds of plants and animals are expendable from the standpoint of ongoing moral interaction. As a matter of fact, human molestation has brought about the extinction (or near extinction) of many species without throwing the natural order into insupportable disarray. That this destruction is compatible with the indefinite survival of moral communities is not surprising inasmuch as animals are not participants in these communities and particular animals are not necessary to the moral agency of the members of these communities. Archetypally, inalienable rights have objects which individuals who are capable of moral agency need in order to exercise this capacity. Consequently, if there are any inalienable environmental rights, they would most likely be persons' rights to a habitable environment, however that may be achieved, not animals' rights to noninterference. Since granting inalienable rights to individual animals is not necessary to maintain an environment that supports moral communities, a moral system that denies these rights would not be self-defeating.

Still, it might be thought that the relations obtaining between animals and the ecosystem are such that moral systems must recognize their rights to noninterference in order not to be self-rescinding. Whereas rights necessary to avert self-defeatism redound to moral agents and proximately secure the viability of moral agency, rights necessary to stave off rescission by design ban permissions that generate moral relations threatening to moral agency. Since rights ordained by this latter criterion of adequacy support moral agency indirectly, animals might conceivably gain such rights in virtue of performing functions essential both to the animals themselves and to the conduct of moral interaction.

It might be tempting to suppose that an animal's performance of its ecological function is indistinguishable from the activities it carries out in order to provide for its own needs. For example, a predator's hunting for food prevents the population of its prey from increasing too much, and in this respect the animal's natural impulses coincide with its helping to stabilize the demographic profile of another animal species. Yet, it is not the case that an animal's pursuit of its ends must contribute to the maintenance of an ecological balance between species.

An animal could be obstructed in its performance of its usual ecological function and yet live an entirely satisfying life. If a huge dome were constructed (assume that it is too large for the animal to reach its circumference once it has been deposited in the middle) in which an animal's natural environment was carefully simulated and in which it could hunt, eat, sleep, and roam about, just as it would in the wild, the animal would not be repressed although its opportunity to carry out certain ecological functions would have been eliminated. Since its artificial environment would have to be stocked with prey, its hunting would not help to keep the population of these animals in check. If anything, the overall population of this species of prey would be increased because the animal would not be killing members of this species in the natural environment and meanwhile additional animals would be raised to supply the replicated environment. Yet, despite this scheme to prevent the animal from playing an ecological role, there is no reason to consider the animal frustrated since it is not being hindered in any of its normal activities.

In contrast, the development of a child's potential for moral agency cannot be separated from her accustomed activities in the way I have distinguished an animal's quotidian behavior from our understanding of this behavior as an ecological role. A child who is frustrated in the development of her ability to function as a moral agent cannot be provided with a substitute structure that will allow her to proceed normally except for the imperceptible omission of her assuming the status of a moral agent. Only through the fictional device of tank life could we glimpse the impact of pure moral agency suppression on moral interaction.

A further difference between my domed animal's experience and a tank dweller's experience is that the former is not under any illusion regarding its life nor does its life generate delusions for the members of the moral community. Although my animal performs no ecological function, it does not erroneously believe it is performing such a function, for no animal correctly believes it occupies an ecological niche. A lion dozing on the plains of Kenya cannot espy a herd of antelope and think, 'I'm not hungry, but I've got to go perform my ecological function.' Animals hunt and have the experience of hunting in my dome. Since they do not also believe that they are helping to maintain an ecological system, they cannot be deluded in this regard, and there is no reason to supply them with result machines to compensate for their disabilities. Furthermore, since their captors have created their artificial environment and service it regularly, neither are they confused about which animals are ecologically active. Indeed, if a moral decision ever turned on the distinction between ecological contribution and ecological superfluity, doming animals would, if anything, help to solve the problem.

Ultimately, it is because animals cannot share in moral interaction—they are limited to profiting from others' adherence to moral principles—that moral systems are not obliged to guarantee their interests through inalienable rights. Since animals are not moral agents, moral systems that prescribe their suffering and destruction are not self-defeating. Also, since preventing animals from fulfilling their ecological destinies need not thwart their natural impulses and would not obfuscate moral relations, moral systems that do not credit animals with inalienable rights are not self-rescinding. In sum, the contribution animals make to moral interaction stands at too great a remove from this nexus to warrant inalienable rights for them. They are collectively instrumental in maintaining an environment hospitable to moral agents, but no individual animal's survival and well-being is indispensable to moral interaction. It follows that animals have no inalienable rights.

6. The Universality of Inalienable Rights

Strictly speaking, only moral agents and normal children meet the qualifications for inalienable rights. No moral system could deny their rights and not prove self-defeating and self-rescinding. Nevertheless, two forms of moral incompetence pose problems for this position.

All moral agents are morally incompetent while they sleep. Since inalienable rights would be nugatory if their protection lapsed with the onset of night, the moral incompetence of an individual who has the potential for moral agency cannot justify denying his inalienable rights. Though a theory of inalienable rights could not be founded solely on a never activated potential for moral agency, recognition of the moral significance of this potential, both in normal children and in adults, is critical to a theory of inalienable rights.

More troubling are cases of abnormal moral incompetence induced by psychological and physiological illness. If the disease is curable, moral agency will return with health, but if the disease is incurable, the individual will become a permanent moral invalid. Sometimes it is possible to determine whether a morally incompetent individual is only temporarily stricken. Frequently, no reliable prognosis can be made. Because diagnostic procedures are notoriously fallible and because mistaken denial of a person's inalienable rights can be catastrophic, it is necessary to adopt a conservative policy requiring irrefragable proof of irremediable moral incompetence before an individual's inalienable rights can be denied. Thus, the protection of inalienable rights extends to many humans who may never engage in moral relations. Though it is only accidental if all humans qualify for inalienable rights, few humans will ever be rightfully deprived of the protection these rights afford.

6

Permissible Abridgment

Moral systems can permit both *in extremis* abridgments of inalienable rights and punishments that abridge these rights. The rights to life, personal liberty, benign treatment, satisfaction of basic needs, and moral education are inalienable but not absolute. Moreover, the outright denial of some right-holders' inalienable rights is compatible with ongoing, albeit truncated, moral interaction. Since invariant respect for these rights is not necessary to this social mode, it may seem a pedantic technicality to contend that adequate moral systems must recognize them. The abstract contents of moral systems only arouse interest, it could be urged, to the extent that they settle how persons may or may not be treated. But this dismissal is flawed in two respects: it conflates infringing rights with violating them and then exaggerates the rigidity with which moral systems must support individual participation in moral communities. Respect for rights is more complex and moral agents are more adaptable than this line of thought allows.

1. Varieties of Abridgment

Abridgments of inalienable rights may be permissible or impermissible, and the permissible ones may be justified on the basis of the prior conduct of the right-holder or on the basis of independent circumstantial exigencies. Corresponding to these possibilities is an assortment of responses that could be made by persons confronting denials, violations, and infringements of their inalienable rights.[1] To understand the subtleties of rights respect, it is necessary to set out these options schematically and to consider their implications for moral agency.

Acts of self-defense and punishment by incarceration number among the uncontroversial forms of inalienable rights infringement. More suspect cases include deprivation of food and medical services on grounds of scarcity (often shortages are artificial) and capital punishment on grounds of deterrence (it is dubious that execution deters). Whether these latter are infringements or violations is open to debate, but among the clear cases of violations are torturing alleged political dissenters and child abuse. Whereas violations of inalienable rights proceed without regard for the right-holder and to no acceptable purpose, infringements take the right-holder's position into account but find a compelling reason to supersede it. Borderline cases are ones in which the victim's claims may not have been appreciated adequately or in which the reason given for declining to respect an individual's rights is not altogether persuasive. Any moral system must proscribe violations of inalienable rights. Moreover, the presumption against depriving a person of a good secured by an inalienable right is so strong that moral systems can only permit incontestable infringements of these rights. Still, it might be asked how moral systems can allow any infringements since they impair or destroy moral agency in the same ways as violations do.

The notion of a justifiable abridgment of an inalienable right is one of morality's concessions to an imperfect world. People do not instinctively obey the prescriptions of morality, and nature is not always bountiful. To contend with these facts, moral systems must permit, though they cannot prescribe, infringements of inalienable rights. This device is a viable one for moral systems because infringements, as opposed to violations,

Permissible Abridgment

are unavoidable, respect the victim's rights insofar as circumstances allow it, and do not banish the right-holder from the moral community.

To say that moral systems must be neither self-defeating nor self-rescinding is not to demand that they be self-perpetuating. Indeed, the latter requirement is incompatible with the former two since it would necessitate prescriptions which the others rule out. Whereas a self-perpetuating moral system must prescribe throwing some lifeboat occupants overboard if it is the only way to save the others, a moral system which is not self-defeating could not generate this obligation. Moral systems that satisfy the negative criteria of adequacy on which inalienable rights are founded are self-perpetuating only in the weakest sense: they do not direct moral agents to take action which could issue in the cessation of moral interaction, nor do they allow their adherents to act in ways that create moral relations inimical to moral interaction. These moral systems contain no principles through which they could themselves bring about the demise of moral interaction, but they do not pretend to mastery of all the ghastly catastrophes imagination (or perusal of the morning newspaper) can discover.

Nevertheless, adequate moral systems must adopt a stand regarding the problem of conflicting rights—situations in which two or more persons' rights compete for respect—since it arises quite commonly. Crime statistics indicate that assailants are almost constantly pitting their rights against those of their victims, and reports from the world's war fronts complain daily of medical supply shortages which prevent doctors from ministering to the basic needs of all casualties. Though no adequate moral system could be responsible for instigating such conditions, only an incomplete moral system could ignore them. It is incumbent on moral systems, therefore, to show how permissions to abridge inalienable rights in extreme adversity respect these rights, despite appearances to the contrary.

In extremis conditions, whether they are localized or widespread, often give rise to competition between inalienable rights.[2] In these situations, it is permissible for right-holders to meet their fate stoically. Rather than be complicit in abridging anyone else's rights, they may let nature take its course, or they may let a malevolent threat be carried out. However, their rights do not oblige them to adopt this passive stance. Some of them may volunteer to sacrifice their own interests in order to ensure respect for others' rights, or some of them may force others to forgo the goods their rights confer in order to prevent the same harm from befalling everyone. These strategies for mitigating overall harm through willing or imposed abridgment can conclude in either of two ways. Depending on which right is at stake (compare the right to life with the right to personal liberty) and the hardiness or susceptibility of the right-holder (compare a typical middle-class American's being deprived of food for two days with a famine victim's being deprived of nourishment for two additional days), an abridgment of an inalienable right may destroy the right-holder outright, or it may temporarily impair his ability to conduct himself with due regard for moral concerns. Which of these outcomes is likely to transpire and the number of victims likely to be claimed dictate the form of respect that can be accorded the victim's (or victims') rights and the extent to which moral relations can be sustained.

The most auspicious situations in which inalienable rights must be infringed are those in which the infringement is not immediately life-threatening and is limited to a single right-holder. Recalling my hypothetical straitened society in which members respect one another's right to satisfaction of basic needs by cooperating to gather food for a communal meal, it can be seen how a person whose rights are infringed can remain integrated in the network of moral relations.[3] Occasionally, through no one's fault, minimally adequate portions can be provided for only nine of the ten members of the group, and the tenth individual must choose between respecting others' rights and trying to satisfy her own needs by taking their allotments. In this situation, her compatriots can plausibly argue that it is rational for her to respect their rights.

Three kinds of argument support the case against this victim's violating her associates' rights. First, she is not being treated unfairly. Whoever is last in line on an unproductive day does not get served. Though there is no satisfactory answer to the question 'why me?' as there is when a person is being punished, the victim understands that she has not been fingered for undeserved mistreatment and that her rights will be respected whenever circumstances permit. Second, her society can offer some compensatory benefit. The work hours of victims of these infringements could be shortened on the following day, or these individuals could be given title to any surplus that might be obtained on the following day. In this way, a society concretely assures its members of its commitment to their rights. Finally, egoistic considerations can be pressed upon her. Since she cannot reasonably expect a more satisfactory life in exile from her society, it behooves her to resist the temptation to violate others' rights. Conducting herself morally is in her own interest.

Infringements of inalienable rights are by definition justified, and the justifications are available to the victim. Rights can be respected, on the one hand, by refraining from interfering with or assisting the right-holder in the requisite way or, on the other hand, by justifying refusal to do so through the use of fair procedures and through appeal to compelling reasons. Moreover, when circumstantial exigency rather than the right-holder's offense justifies the infringement, the society's respect for the victim's right can be further affirmed through compensatory measures. Both the provision of a justification and the offer of compensation appeal to the victim's egoistic, as well as his moral, inclinations. The justification addresses his intellect and his *amour propre* asking him to govern himself rationally and not to forsake his personal ideals while the offer of compensation enhances the attractions of continued restraint. Though persons cannot be obligated to acquiesce in these arrangements, societal respect for infringed inalienable rights can enable the victim's interest in conducting himself with dignity and regard for others to dominate his urge to relieve the proximate cause of his distress.

Still, at the opposite end of the spectrum of infringements lie some intractable cases, ones in which the deaths of right-holders are inevitable. Lifeboats or critical medications may be in short supply, or a maniac may be brandishing a weapon at a captive crowd. Whatever the source of the predicament, respect for inalienable rights among the victims reduces to impartiality. If some persons are to be saved, those who are to die must be chosen fairly; but, since they are about to die, they cannot be compensated. Thus, these individuals confront the most dreadful future, cannot be appeased, and are liable to panic. Though people have sometimes behaved with unruffled aplomb and unwavering conformity to the highest personal ideals in the face of certain and horrible death, the annals of disaster behavior are replete with shameless groveling and frenzied attempts to escape as well. Since the sacrifice exacted in this sort of situation is one that morality cannot prescribe and that egoism usually counsels strongly against, the collapse of voluntary moral relations impends.

If the strongest members of a threatened group use force to protect themselves at the expense of weaker individuals, their action is understandable but not morally justified. Despite the inevitability of some right-holders' untimely deaths, persons can respect one another's inalienable rights by accepting a fair procedure to decide whom to sacrifice. But since those selected cannot be obligated to submit to the group's decision, it may be necessary to coerce their compliance. Because these situations accommodate a vestigial form of respect for inalienable rights, a distinction can be drawn between rightful and wrongful deployments of force. However, because the designated victims remain free to resist the outcome of the group's deliberations and because only the most exalted personal ideals could provide egoistic grounds for submission, the crisis has no satisfactory resolution.

Some predicaments land the protagonists in a moral shadow world of constrained but antagonistic permissions. Circumstances are not so tumultuous that respect for rights is altogether impossible. Consequently, the persons chosen to be sacrificed cannot complain that their fellow victims have violated their rights provided that appropriate decision procedures have been observed. They can only lament the dire straits in which they find themselves. To the extent that right-holders can

Permissible Abridgment

take consolation in the fact that their fellows have not wronged them and can call upon a firm commitment to a demanding personal ideal, they may be inspired to embrace their sacrificial role. But, if rage at the pitilessness of fortune seizes them, they may fiercely resist their lot or sullenly submit to superior force. At the edge of the possibility of moral intercourse, individual psychology supplants moral responsibility and determines whether or not a modicum of moral order can persist without the aid of force.

Since persons cannot be expected to act purely out of a sense of duty when their inalienable rights are in jeopardy, a society that occasionally finds it necessary to infringe a member's inalienable rights must rely on egoistic incentives to keep the victim from bolting. As long as infringements are seldom necessary or compensation for them does not exceed the society's means, moral relations are stable. But if infringements become prevalent or compensation is impossible, moral relations are prone to deteriorate. To the extent that self-interest can be enlisted as a kind of motivational overdrive when abridgment of an individual's inalienable rights is permissible, a moral community can contend with infringements of its members' rights. However, when self-interest clearly dictates resistance on the part of victimized right-holders and only compassion for others argues for submission, the society's environment, natural or social, is so inhospitable that normally self-regarding agents could be expected to shun moral compliance. At this point, respect for rights pales into a formal justice too paltry to galvanize the allegiance of moral agents. Force alone can be relied on to secure a moral order.

2. The Wrong of Denial

Moral communities can absorb inalienable rights infringements insofar as self-interest can intercede to sustain moral agency or legitimate force can be interjected as an interim measure. Why, then, can moral systems not deny some persons' inalienable rights and substitute egoistic inducements to moral conformity or enforce it with sanctions?

Presumably there are some forms of inalienable rights denial that could not be offset by egoistic incentives. For instance, nothing could entice a person into agreeing to pointless subjection to constant torture, and, since nothing worse could happen to anyone, no threat would be persuasive. Nevertheless, the fact that some long-lived societies have permitted slavery suggests that a moral system's exclusion of some persons' inalienable rights could be innocuous from the standpoint of maintaining moral intercourse.

Historically, moral communities have subscribed to moral codes that conveniently denied the inalienable rights of conquered peoples. These communities have not, as a rule, been subject to quicker dissolution than ones that espoused moral systems acknowledging all right-holders. But to think that this fact somehow certifies the adequacy of these moral systems is to misunderstand the criteria of adequacy from which inalienable rights are derived. The reason for rejecting self-defeating and self-rescinding moral systems is not a doomsday prediction that they will terminate moral interaction. On the contrary, a moral community inhabiting a commodious environment and graced by adept political leadership might believe in the righteousness of sundry atrocities and yet prosper. Still, its moral code would be deficient regardless of its longevity since this moral system would contain principles capable of stopping moral interaction, principles which moral agents could not properly be held responsible for upholding.

Slave owners must rationalize denying their slaves' inalienable rights by denying that these individuals are capable of moral agency and thus that they are qualified to possess the right to personal liberty which would proscribe their subservience. The institution's characteristic perfidy is that this contempt for slaves may not be wholly unfounded. The humiliation and invasiveness of slavery can degrade individuals so profoundly that their qualifications for inalienable rights may indeed become suspect. Abjectly submissive slaves who have

Permissible Abridgment 151

internalized their masters' ideology and have come to approve their subordinate status are not unknown. They believe themselves to be inferior, and it is possible that in some cases a lifetime of dependency and abuse has suppressed their moral potential beyond recovery. A moral system that condones slavery's systematic degradation authorizes creation of a subpopulation composed of persons who could not assume the duties of responsible moral agents should the occasion arise. If this result is effected, the moral system has been instrumental in generating an artificial need for authority figures which could needlessly curtail moral interaction. But if, as is quite likely, some slaves emerge as capable moral agents, these individuals belie the affirmation of their incompetence upon which the moral system's hierarchical principles rest. Whether such moral systems are despised for their hypocrisy or for their self-rescinding potential, moral agents are justified in rejecting them.

In contrast to an abjectly submissive slave, a tactically submissive slave is not gulled by her mistreatment. She knows that she is capable of moral agency and that her inalienable rights ought to be respected, but she feigns acquiescence to protect herself or to conceal plans for revolt. Her behavior is constrained by negative egoistic factors—she pretends to accept her enslavement in order to avoid worse affliction—but her egoistic designs do not second the moral system that denies her inalienable rights as egoistic considerations do moral systems permitting infringements.

Since coercion serving to maintain slavery is not based on compelling reasons and fair procedures and therefore does not respect inalienable rights, persons subject to it are wronged by fellow right-holders. Accordingly, there is no reason for them to take pride in compliance with their oppression. At variance with this is the perspective of adherents of moral systems that are sometimes obliged to allow rights infringements. They may congratulate themselves for salvaging what moral relations are possible under adverse conditions. Furthermore, through surveillance and terror, a society denying slaves' inalienable rights seeks to confine their egoistic calculations to the narrow problem of avoiding death and agony.[4] Unlike moral systems countenancing rights infringements, these moral systems would contradict their own tenets if they sought to secure their victims' compliance by promising eventual respect for these persons' rights. Though the need for caution and stealth may postpone a slave population's liberation indefinitely, weakness cannot finally eradicate the egoistic case for rebellion. Only freedom can afford them safety and the opportunity for self-realization. In denying some persons' inalienable rights, then, slave societies apply force devoid of moral justification. Adequate moral systems are incapable of such brutality.

Moral systems can tolerate infringements of inalienable rights because these abridgments neither show disrespect for rights nor alienate right-holders to a point where compliance can only be seen as a tactic for avoiding worse oppression. But to condone denial of inalienable rights is to allow attendant violations which arbitrarily injure the unrecognized right-holder and justify him in resisting moral relations as prescribed by this moral system. Inalienable rights, whether recognized and honored, recognized and infringed, or denied but cherished, are necessary for moral relations. It is precisely because abridgment of inalienable rights rarely succeeds in degrading persons to the point of believing they are incapable of moral agency and therefore unqualified for inalienable rights that moral relations can survive unavoidable evils and, even, some unconscionable outrages.

3. The Problem of Enforcement

Whereas *in extremis* infringements are justified by terrible adventitious circumstances—nature or alien agents menace right-holders—the reason for punishing wrongdoers is internal to moral communities. Consequently, it may seem that the moral systems these communities uphold must be defective if they cannot prevent their own adherents from going astray. Of course, a moral system that fostered vice only to punish it would be inadmissible. But since persons cannot be unfailingly impelled to follow moral dicta, no moral system can secure perfect compliance. Thus, the problem of enforcement within moral communities is not one that moral systems can eliminate.

Ever since Locke's declaration that the state's consolidated coercive powers are the appropriate remedy for the "inconveniences" of the state of nature, fundamental rights have been widely regarded as inseparable from state enforcement.[5] Yet, it is not immediately obvious how inalienable rights and enforcement are related nor why there should be a state to assume the burden of enforcement. Complex and elusive as the interpenetration between the moral realm and the political realm is (certainly, no comprehensive attempt to sort out these issues will be made here), the theory of inalienable rights contributes an account of a fundamental tie between these two spheres. Briefly, because rights possession is trifling unless rights assertion goes with it and because right-holders are not competent to exercise their rights in all requisite ways, an agency—the state—must supply this lack.

Despite substantial disagreement about the precise dimensions of the entitlements conferred by rights, there is rarely doubt as to whether right-holders are entitled to assert their rights. Pressing claims on the strength of a right may be selfish or ill-advised, and responding to farfetched claims may be a nuisance. Nevertheless, the right-holder's liberty to stand on his right—to oppose its abridgment and to demand recognition as a victim in the wake of abridgment—is hard to controvert. Without this implicit liberty, right-holders would be consigned to passivity and rights would reduce to their correlative duties.

In thus legitimating self-defense, rights inject the problem of enforcement, that is, the problem of what persons may do to secure their rights, into the moral sphere. Confining enforcement to warding off aggression in progress would constrict it unduly. Since frail individuals would be bereft of any defensive capability, their liberty to assert their rights against aggressors would be practically void. Furthermore, this understanding of self-defense would ignore the harm done to the victims of rights violations. Having failed to avert aggression, victims would lack any recourse. If enforcement of rights is not to depend entirely on arbitrary differences in the maneuvering capabilities of right-holders, and if enforcement is to extend to acknowledgment of the claims of victims, it must include punishment. Punishment evens the contest between prospective assailants and their would-be victims and provides a mechanism through which the wrongs suffered by victims can be acknowledged.

Broadly construed, the liberty of self-defense not only frees right-holders to fend off assailants but also frees them to take measures to prevent attacks on their rights. When penalties for rights violations are fixed so that incurring them is unacceptable to virtually all agents, when the declaration that these penalties will be imposed is credible, and when the alternatives to violating rights are acceptable, sanctions render rights violations ineligible. Most people who are subject to properly calibrated sanctions in a social setting conducive to their operation do not yearn to commit crimes, only to be restrained after they anticipate the punishment. Rather, the forbidden actions never occur to most of these individuals as options to be seriously considered.[6] Accordingly, institutionalized sanctions constitute a system of preemptive defense that protects those who are capable of mounting their own defenses in moments of danger as well as those who are helpless.

Yet, since it is impossible to guarantee that no one will ever find the risk of punishment preferable to available alternatives, rights violations are inevitable, and provisions must be made for postinfraction rights enforcement. When pernicious conditions make abridgment of someone's right unavoidable, the beneficiaries of this sacrifice are usually grateful and sometimes lionize their savior. However, criminals are generally loathe to take responsibility for the wrong they have done and to recognize their victims as such. Moreover, if compensating the victim of a justified abridgment is fitting, compensating the victim of a violation must be insufficient since this latter individual has been deprived not only of the object of his right but also of the respect due his right. Beyond securing the credibility of preemptive defenses, then, inflicting punishment must give expression to the community's sense of the victim's redoubled aggrievement.[7] This twofold function is evident in the restraints we place on punishment. Whereas the purposes of preemptive defense recommend setting the severity of punishments according to an amalgam of the intensity of the desire to prevent the crime and the intensity of the desire to commit it, the purposes of victim recognition require that the punishment be proportional to the crime.

Supposing that the assertibility of rights argues for their enforceability and that enforcement comprises the dual thrust sketched above, rights deployment poses a series of problems revolving around the relation between individually held rights and state enforcement of them. To protect individuals adequately, inalienable rights must authorize right-holders to resist violations of their rights. Since promulgating and levying punishment is an extension of this defensive liberty, it appears that this elaborated mode of enforcement must also number among the right-holder's prerogatives. However, attributing this liberty exclusively to the right-holder provides a ready excuse for crime when it is disguised as punishment and incites criminals to murder their victims as a means of eluding punishment for lesser malfeasance. Yet, despite these drawbacks, it is not clear how enforcement can be detached from the right-holder.

For the same reasons that inalienable rights are nontransferable, the liberties to exercise these rights are immune to transfer. To lose these liberties is to be obligated to submit to treatment destructive of one's moral agency regardless of whether anyone else is entitled to inflict it; however, because moral systems countenancing obligatory passivity with respect to the objects of inalienable rights are self-defeating, no acceptable moral system can allow its adherents to become playthings for wanton cruelty or uncommon obtuseness. It follows that liberties to press claims predicated on inalienable rights are inalienable.

Important as this result obviously is for the security of inalienable right-holders, it is also perplexing. As it stands, it seems to bar private cooperative enforcement of rights along with state enforcement. Nonvictimized right-holders cannot intervene to enforce victims' rights except on the dubious pretext that every crime that goes unpunished is a threat to every right-holder. Moreover, since the rights in question are inalienable and so too are the liberties to assert these rights, the remedy of voluntarily transferring enforcement liberties to a centralized agency—consenting to join civil society, in the parlance of classical contract theories—is not available. Worse still, it is arguable that, for all its deterrent advantages, institutionalizing punishment improperly severs the convict's suffering from the wrong she has committed and from the victim who is owed recognition. State administered penal sanctions are divorced from their source in rights exercise, but private enforcers may be unable to establish a convincing deterrent or to bring their assailants to justice. Yet, if the prospect of my rights being violated is what justifies me (and only me) in asserting my rights anticipatorily by announcing that I will punish violators, and if the fact of my rights having been violated is what justifies me (and no one else) in punishing the guilty party, and if neither of these forms of rights assertion is transferable, each right-holder seems doomed to remain a state unto himself.

Fortunately, this prognosis overlooks a critical element of the moral situation rights establish. Though liberties to assert rights are indeed nontransferable, this claim does not imply that right-holders can exercise these liberties only on their own behalf or that they must empower an agent to exercise their liberties before anyone else may assume this burden. A guardian, acting as proxy for an incapacitated right-holder, may exercise these liberties in the interests of the disabled right-holder.[8] Consequently, state intervention in the arena of inalienable rights enforcement is vindicated if inalienable right-holders are not competent to enforce their rights individually or through private cooperation but the state is competent to perform this function.

4. The Injustice of Private Enforcement

Punishment infringes inalienable rights but ought not violate them. Any liberty to punish rights-violators must, therefore, be circumscribed by inalienable rights. Though these rights do not block punishment altogether, they do bar punishing the innocent and imposing excessive penalties. Of course, no one is clairvoyant, and this epistemological predicament precludes airtight guarantees that only the guilty will be punished and only to the right degree. Nevertheless, trial and sentencing procedures can be devised to minimize judicial error without acquitting all but the most brazen criminals. To be justified in inflicting punishment, then, an enforcer must decide whom to punish and how much punishment to impose using fair procedures which allow the accused individual to defend herself. Adherence to these procedures coupled with close and sympathetic attention to the accused's defense absolves rights-enforcers of charges that they have violated others' rights while exercising theirs.

Now, it is clear that individuals, proceeding alone or in concert, can scrupulously comply with the judicial principles others' rights imply, but it is also undeniable that such conscientiousness is liable to falter. Whether understandable anger at their own wrongful affliction bestirs persons to relax these standards or seductive opportunities to gain by pretending to punish wrongdoers corrupt them, right-holders will sometimes compromise judicial rectitude. Still, since such lapses would not necessarily be ubiquitous, it may seem alarmist to declare individuals incompetent to enforce their own rights.

To see why the possible rarity of private enforcement abuse cannot justify leaving enforcement to individuals, it is necessary first to recollect the origins of enforcement liberties. They are intended, on the one hand, to obviate rights violations through preemptive defense and, on the other hand, to prevent compounding the initial wrong of violations with the further wrong of victim neglect. In short, enforcement prerogatives aim to ensure respect for inalienable rights. But because respect for these rights may appear to violate them and violations may be concealed, private enforcement is inadequate to the task.

Right-holders are rarely mistaken about whether they are enjoying the prime benefits to which their inalienable rights entitle them. Introspection readily discovers intimidation, pain, and the like. But right-holders may easily err in ascribing blame for violations, as when a person inadvertantly punishes an innocent party, and they are prone to misclassify infringements as violations, as when a defendant or convict sincerely imputes rights violations to legitimate enforcement measures. Even under ideal enforcement arrangements, appearance may not coincide with reality. Guilty defendants have reason to disavow their crimes while judges' unconscious motives may contaminate otherwise meticulous proceedings. Nevertheless, just as avoidable slavery or malnutrition violates inalienable rights, avoidable judicial error in convicting, sentencing, and punishing violates these rights, too. Only when persons have reason to believe that they are not, as judges, violating others' rights and are not, as defendants, subject to violations is it the case that enforcement does not violate inalienable rights.

For defendants and convicts to be satisfied that their rights are secure, enforcers must conduct themselves in a manner which enables defendants and convicts to distinguish enforcement from murder, kidnapping, and torture. A person who reasonably believes that her rights are being or are about to be violated is justified in counterattacking. Accordingly, enforcers must assure their fellow right-holders that they have taken all reasonable precautions to avoid error in convicting, sentencing, and punishing. In sum, it is not enough for an enforcer to follow fair procedures and to maintain an impartial attitude; in addition, the enforcer must provide evidence of doing so sufficient

Permissible Abridgment 159

to persuade a reasonable defendant or convict that she is not free to obstruct her proceedings. Otherwise, enforcement not only violates defendants' and convicts' liberties of self-defense by preventing them from discerning when they may exercise these liberties forcefully, but it also precipitates defensive stratagems on the part of defendants and convicts which in turn may stymie victimized right-holders' enforcement liberties.

It is unnecessary to assume that persons will take advantage of their enforcement liberties to deliberately violate inalienable rights to see that private enforcement is untenable. The most instructive case for study is that of the innocent individual convicted of a crime by another individual exercising her enforcement rights. Three explanations of this miscarriage of justice must be considered: 1) the enforcer used unjust trial procedures; 2) the enforcer's prejudices against the defendant overwhelmed procedural safeguards; and 3) the ascertainable facts of the case pointed to the defendant's guilt and provided negligible evidence of her innocence. When an individual is tried by another individual, none of these explanations can be ruled out.

Whatever the accused individual's initial convictions about adequate procedural controls may have been, it is reasonable for her to question these beliefs upon realizing that they have permitted a false verdict to be reached. Accordingly, even if the defendant and her judge begin by agreeing to procedures and follow them assiduously, the wrongly convicted defendant may retrospectively find fault with them. But if she cannot determine which rule or combination of rules perverted justice, she may shift her attention to her judge's psychology. Since the defendant cannot apprise herself of a self-possessed judge's real attitudes toward her, it is reasonable for her to wonder whether this individual's outwardly calm and astute demeanor has masked a vengeful hatred so powerful that conviction was preordained. Of course, the innocent convict has no way of confirming or disconfirming suspicions of this kind. Finally, she may suppose that the circumstances surrounding her case were too Byzantine ever to be unraveled and therefore that no judge, however scrupulous and neutral, would have acquitted her. But, once again, it is impossible for the defendant to test this hypothesis, and, in the absence of decisive reasons controverting the other two hypotheses, there is no reason for her to blame her conviction on the intricacy and obscurity of her case. Thus, innocent individuals wrongly but not necessarily wrongfully convicted by others are entitled to complain that they have been snared by illicit procedures or malicious administration.

Notice, moreover, that guilty defendants who have pleaded not-guilty are entitled to lodge the same objections. To respect a defendant's inalienable rights, it is not sufficient that a judge announce the correct verdict.[9] The judge must arrive at her decision following fair procedures and unswayed by personal bias. Though it is not wrong in the abstract that a guilty person be convicted, a judge who dispenses with trial procedures or unleashes her enmity on the defendant violates this individual's rights, her guilt notwithstanding.

If individuals are empowered to enforce their own rights, their judicial decisions and the accusations which may be leveled against their proceedings are sheltered from scrutiny. Either judges regard themselves as fair, or they know themselves to be shamming. In either case, they would accept only like-minded arbitrators if they would allow their enforcement activities to be reviewed at all. A judge who does not sincerely believe she has found the culprit, it must be remembered, undoubtedly intends to conceal her own vice. In light of this possibility, defendants would be foolish to accept referees proposed by their judges. Likewise, from the standpoint of honest judges, convicts, regardless of their claims to innocence, are presumed to be guilty and therefore cannot be trusted to select arbitrators sympathetic to legitimate punishment. This stalemate of mutual distrust is what renders individuals incompetent to enforce their own rights: only convictions of confessed criminals are authoritative; all others are open to dispute.

Still, it might be urged that the state is a needlessly extreme solution for the problem of nonauthoritative trials. Not only does the state fail to improve on private enforcement by eliminating the problem of the innocent convict—nothing can prevent judicial mistakes; but also procedures for selecting mutually acceptable arbitrators could circumvent the impasse depicted above—private appeals could be instituted. Private enforcement abuse might be curbed, and mutual distrust between judges and defendants might be relieved through mechanisms for appointing arbitrators whom both parties would have chosen if neither had known the other's preference and for adopting procedural rules which both parties would have picked if neither had known the other's views. However, these provisions for blind selection of arbitrators and procedures would satisfy the litigants about the propriety of the subsequent review only to the extent that they are confident about their own choices.

Mutual distrust alleviated, self-doubt may surface. If a judge's good-faith decision is reversed or if an innocent convict is not cleared, the disappointed individual may entertain second thoughts about the wisdom of her commitment to the arbitration process. Here, too, the innocent convict can attribute an unsatisfactory outcome to bad procedures, a partial arbitrator, or the opacity of her case. Only punishments imposed on innocent convicts who are sure that their deliberations about who should adjudicate and how she should proceed were free of error, and exonerations bestowed on convicts whose judges are equally secure in their acceptance of the review plan will be authoritative; the remainder will be clouded by doubts about the rectitude of the proceedings. Though the objections of guilty convicts seem to be quelled by the proposed appeals measures—their ostensible self-doubts are all too likely to be dishonestly self-serving—innocent convicts and self-proclaimed victims of penal brutality who get no satisfaction from these proceedings seem entitled to press for further investigation of their cases.

Despite these difficulties, someone might object that my observations do not exhibit any inescapable violations plaguing a system of private enforcement. That innocent defendants may reasonably suspect their prosecutor-judges of conducting debased trials and that convicts may reasonably suspect their jailers of aggravating their sentences does not prove that their doubts are well founded and that their rights are being violated. A warranted suspicion of a violation is not a violation. Unless we ascribe rank stupidity or vile duplicity to enforcers, the objection concludes, there is no reason to suppose that private enforcement conceals anything untoward.

The trouble with private enforcement is not merely that it cultivates reflexive skepticism but rather that this skepticism is symptomatic of this system's inability to provide right-holders with adequate assurance that their rights are not vulnerable to undetectable violations. The problem is structural, not episodic. Private enforcers, through no fault of their own, cannot exercise their rights without leaving innocent convicts and many prisoners in doubt as to whether they are entitled to obstruct the proceedings. Perhaps the most perspicuous way to formulate the problem is to say that any system of private enforcement, whether it provides appeals opportunities or not, must commit a damning lie of omission. As a result of the barriers that divide individuals and the urgency of the interests that are at stake, private enforcers are debarred from communicating the information necessary to defuse other right-holders' defensive liberties. In light of the paramount importance of basic rights protections, uncertainty justifies resistance. Since a person cannot be expected to submit to violence on the chance that the aggressor has a good reason for her conduct, the ambiguity inherent in private enforcement constitutes a provocation to reciprocal violence rather than a legitimate judicial proceeding.

Needless to say, enforcement systems need not be designed so as to convince every right-holder, no matter how meretricious her quarrels with it, that her basic rights will be respected should she ever be indicted. Yet, an enforcement system that does not afford defendants and convicts all reasonable guarantees of its steadfast respect for basic rights thereby violates these rights. Not only must right-holders be provided with channels through which they can assert their rights and receive a fair hearing when they are accused or declared guilty of wrongdoing, but also restraints on enforcement agents along with institutions that procure serious consideration for worthwhile reform proposals must be incorporated into the system. Unless such provisions are made, enforcement remains a standoff between competing liberties of self-defense. Once the requisite guarantees have been implemented, enforcers gain a moral power to try suspects and to sentence convicts while right-holders become morally liable to these proceedings.[10]

5. Enforcement and the State

For judicial decisions to be authoritative, judges must be regarded as impartial executors of fair procedural principles and substantive regulations. Yet, human fallibility being what it is, this standard can only be approximated. The pivotal problem of enforcement, then, is how to maximize authoritative judicial pronouncements, in other words, how to respect rights in the context of enforcement. Judges, the procedures they observe, and the sanctions they impose must somehow be certified. With respect to procedures and penalties, tradition—continuous adherence to a set of rules over time—supports their reliability and appropriateness. Provided they have not been foisted autocratically upon an unwilling populace and also that they have been adjusted to correct flaws discovered in them, rules prove themselves in practice. The question of administration is parallel. When judges are chosen on the strength of their qualifications and when these individuals are answerable to those who may come before them, a presumption of their propriety is established. Plainly, any enforcement system that can nurture a coherent but reformable body of judicial tradition, that can win a consensus about the suitability of punishments, and that is organized to install and impeach judicial officials amounts to a rudimentary state.

Still, it must be conceded that the precautions of public enforcement do not rule out the possibility that innocent persons will be declared guilty and will be punished. As a result, the difference between private enforcement and its public counterpart may seem to be a quantitative difference in the probability of being convicted though innocent rather than a qualitative difference in the position of innocent convicts under the two systems. But this is a misapprehension. For an innocent person who is convicted by a private rights-enforcer can properly regard her punishment as a violation of her rights, whereas a similarly situated person who is convicted by properly constituted public enforcement institutions must view her misfortune as an infringement.

This difference is explained by the fact that under the punctilious state, prejudicial procedures and inept or malevolent judicial conduct cease to be highly plausible explanations of erroneous convictions and excessive sentences. Because public enforcement institutions are guided by tested rules and are implemented by screened officials whose comportment is subject to review on appeal, it is unreasonable for an innocent convict who has exhausted the remedies available to her to blame the law or its administrators. The only remaining explanation of her plight is the impenetrability of her case, that is, the impossibility of discerning her innocence given the mischances of circumstances.[11] Now, since this is the most plausible account of an innocent person's condemnation by public enforcement agencies, her situation is analogous to that of a person who is fairly deprived of food in a famine. Everything possible has been done to ensure respect for her rights, but circumstances have conspired to prevent the right-holder from obtaining the benefit to which she is entitled. Under these conditions, abridgment is unavoidable and, though unfortunate, is not culpable.

To achieve the good of rights respect, rights enforcement must be guaranteed to all, and it must be generally known to be impartial and fair. Under modern social conditions, these desiderata can only be achieved by the state.[12] Admittedly, state officials can abandon right-holders whom they arbitrarily deem unworthy, and they can deliver biased proceedings and barbaric sentences while disingenuously protesting that they are enforcing rights. The difference between public enforcement and private enforcement is emphatically not that the former is incorruptible but rather that the latter cannot secure respect for rights. However conscientious individuals may be when enforcing their rights, their decisions are not authoritative in a critical range of cases and thus needlessly abridge inalienable rights. Despite its vulnerability to all sorts of sabotage, properly constituted state enforcement is the only approximation to enforcement omnipotence and objectivity to which the members of a society can entrust their rights. Under the state, the position of right-holders is transformed: whereas they are automatic victims of structural rights violations under private enforcement, they have hope of receiving justice at the hands of the state.

Though enforcement liberties are inalienable, a state must be empowered to exercise these rights on behalf of right-holders in order to prevent these individuals' enforcement activities from violating the very rights they aim to secure. With a legitimate judicial authority in operation and with a social and economic environment that supports it, promulgated sanctions usually deflect the very impetus to violate rights. Thus, everyone's primary rights are protected, and no one's defensive liberties are violated. Still, the problem of inflicting punishment when these defenses fail needs to be explored since it is not clear that the state's monopolization of this responsibility does not usurp a function residing in the individual.

6. The Imposition of Punishment

If their rights are violated, right-holders are entitled to demand acknowledgment of their victimization. Multiform as this acknowledgement may be, refusing a victim this solace is a further violation of her right unless there are overriding circumstances. In addition to its defensive function, we have seen, punishment respects the rights of victims in the aftermath of violations. However, state-inflicted punishment may seem inadequate to this purpose since it removes the criminal's subjection to punishment from the commission of the wrong that occasions it. In contrast, a criminal whose victim punishes her can hardly forget why her inalienable rights are being abridged. Though she may feel no repentance (indeed, she may feel defiance), she is obliged to confront the outrage of her victim who in turn has the satisfaction of seeing her tormenter suffer.

One weakness of this rather primitive picture of punishment as reciprocal suffering is its indifference to convicts' rights. Since these individuals' inalienable rights are not forfeit and only infringements commensurate to their crimes are justifiable, penal sanctions can spark the same sort of distrust that taints private judicial proceedings. If a convict believes she is being subjected to sporadic hectoring or routines contrived to render her punishment excessively harsh, she may reasonably surmise that penal officers are violating her rights. Of course, securing prisoners' rights is a notoriously vexing problem, and no monitoring system ever seems stringent enough fully to allay convicts' worries. But what is important here is that no offender could trust her victim to confine her punishment to the terms of the sentence and, furthermore, that no informal supervisory measures could adequately offset these suspicions. For the same reason that victims of rights violations cannot conduct authoritative trials, they cannot inflict punishment irreproachably.

The temptation to think that the victims of rights violations must play some official role in punishment is rooted in quotidian social intercourse. In this context, persons occasionally wrong each other in minor ways, and these disruptions are handled through apologies and efforts to make it up to the victim, on the part of the wrongdoer, and through forgiveness, on the part of the wronged individual. Persistent or exceptionally offensive infractions may lead to the wrongdoer's social ostracism, but generally persons reach a mutual understanding that smooths their association. Inasmuch as institutionalized punishment is modeled to some extent on this form of social interchange, it may be tempting to transpose all of the details. But because rights violations are not the same order of infraction as the social gaffe or the moral blunder, there are important differences between the social mechanisms for handling these problems. Though a rights-violator may be acquainted with her victim, her offense, in all but the most exceptional cases, permanently estranges them. Violations of inalienable rights are so vile that the normal cycle of repentance and forgiveness rarely reconciles individuals who had not previously shared deep ties of affection and often fails to reconcile those who had such bonds.

This unnegotiable estrangement explains why conceiving of punishment as the victim's cathartic infliction of proportionate suffering on her assailant is misguided. A victim's visiting suffering upon a wrongdoer can be dismissed as gratuitous vengeance unless it can normally be expected to elicit the wrongdoer's contrition and facilitates their reconciliation. The malefactor's remorse is the usual form of acknowledgment bestowed upon victims of minor offenses. However, punishment cannot extract remorse from rights-violators, and the harm of an inalienable rights violation is so devastating that victims need not be mollified by violators' professions of repentance, even supposing them to be genuine. Though the state is impotent in the face of criminal obstinacy and the unmitigable revulsion victims may feel for their assailants, it can respect the rights of victims, that is, it can acknowledge their victimization, by punishing rights-violators. Where interpersonal reconciliation almost invariably falters, symbolic rights respect in the form of the state's penal rituals is the only available substitute for the substantive rights respect of heartfelt regret and reform.[13] Thus, punishment does not mediate relations between rights-violators and their victims. Instead, it embodies societal acknowledgment of the wrong suffered by one of its members.

Sometimes punishment is justified from the convict's rather than from her victim's point of view. It may be said that, in order to respect the guilty individual's rights and to allow her to discharge the wrong she has done, the community must punish her.[14] This somewhat mystical treatment exerts a persistent attraction because it offers an explanation of why punishment is not a violation of the convict's rights: punishment gives the convict what she really wants by redressing the moral imbalance she has created, thus enabling her to return to the moral community in equilibrium with it. However, by looking at the problem of rights respect from the standpoint of the victim's entitlement to acknowledgment, the permissibility of punishment can be established without adverting to occult expulsions from and paternalistic receptions back into moral communities. Punishment is justified because, under normal social conditions, it is the only way a victim's rights can be respected. The victim's rights conflict with the convict's rights, but the victim has a stronger claim. Hence, punishment merely infringes the convict's rights.

At this point, it might seem that defending punishment as a form of respect for the rights of victims proves too much, for it is obligatory to respect their rights and this obligation would require infringing the perpetrator's rights. Construed in this way, punishment seems to prescribe conduct that adequate moral systems can only permit. However, this charge overlooks the state's dual responsibility in enforcing rights and the counterbalance to the victim's rights that the convict's rights exert.

To function as the convict's as well as the victim's agent and to ensure that neither's rights are violated, the state must regard judicial sentences as provisional, that is, as permissible to execute yet permissible to countermand. The official pardon institutionalizes the latter option; it empowers an officer to cut through a welter of encrusted law and entropic bureaucracy to give preference to a convict's rights. Though officials grant pardons sparingly in order not to undermine the state's enforcement authority and hardly ever grant them for reasons of mercy, the existence of this unrestricted discretionary power testifies not only to the possibility that mistakes in the course of regular enforcement procedures may later come to light but also to the possibility that a legally correct verdict and sentence can rightfully be overturned.[15] A person who is guilty of the crime for which she has been convicted deserves to be punished, and yet punishment is not inflicted without moral reluctance, or even trepidation. Calls for rehabilitation programs in prisons and the executioner's traditional request for forgiveness evidence this ambivalence about subjecting persons to abridgments of their inalienable rights. This seaminess we associate with punishment despite the convict's deserts is the intuitive counterpart of the permissibility of pardoning a convict despite her victim's rights. Though it is not wrong to punish rights violators, punishment is not a morally translucent undertaking and is not obligatory.

The importance of not conflating the realistic good of respecting inalienable rights with the fantastic good of invariantly according right-holders the objects of their inalienable rights cannot be stressed too much. To say that rights respect is a good is not to say that, when this good is achieved, no one will ever be deprived of any of the objects of his rights contrary to his will. Rather, it affirms that no one's rights will be neglected, while conceding that various kinds of circumstances—ranging from natural disasters to human waywardness—can necessitate infringement. The benefit conferred by inalienable rights respect couples the individual's prerogative of rights assertion with the state's provisions against wronging and abandoning right-holders. Ordinarily, this combination secures the objects of these rights. Still, because respecting inalienable rights is not equivalent to the unattainable goal of respecting absolute rights, the former accommodates state enforcement: the suffering it may inflict on persons found guilty of violating inalienable rights as well as the bewilderment and resentment of victims whose assailants may be freed.

7. State Implementation of Subsistence Rights

The right to benign treatment, insofar as it requires provision of medical relief for acute pain, and the right to satisfaction of basic needs, inasmuch as it requires provision of essential goods, resist the approach to enforcement sketched above. That each person has a right to benign treatment and a right to satisfaction of basic needs entails that every person has a duty to respect these rights by supplying the specified benefits on demand. Yet, it seems an exaggeration to label withholding goods justifiably claimed under these rights a crime since these claims may unduly burden some individuals and since no one can keep abreast of all these claims. Whereas a person can effortlessly and simultaneously respect everyone's rights to noninterference by refraining from aggression, a person may be obliged to devote considerable time to assessing the merits of demands for aid and to bear substantial costs in honoring legitimate claims. Though some philosophers use observations of this sort to contend that there are no basic rights to assistance, I shall take it as established that there are inalienable rights to benign treatment and satisfaction of basic needs and shall ask whether their implementation should be left to individual good will and conscience.[16]

To grasp this issue, it is useful to begin by examining a small and cohesive community with a simple, self-enclosed economy at a primitive stage of development. Voluntary cooperative respect for the rights to benign treatment and satisfaction of basic needs is not unthinkable in this context. The members of the community know each other; hence they know one another's resources and needs, and their frequent contact with one another fosters mutual sympathy. As a result, when a calamity befalls one of their number, they respond automatically by organizing relief. If someone's shelter is struck by lightning and burns, those who have spare building materials contribute what the victim lacks, and everyone who has construction skills helps to erect the new shelter. Both needs and remedies are evident to all. Moreover, hoarders and shirkers are easily exposed and are persuaded to assume their fair share. In a society that is unified and transparent to its members, there is no reason to suppose that respect for the rights to benign treatment and satisfaction of basic needs will be erratic or that respecting these rights will unfairly burden or benefit anyone. Consequently, there is no reason to institute official implementation mechanisms.

The situation of modern postindustrial nation-states hardly resembles the one I have just described. Participants in these societies have family, friends, and associates, but no one's acquaintanceship coincides with the class of prospective claimants. In my simple society, everyone knows every right-holder who might require assistance because this community is small and no one is aware of events beyond its boundaries. Persons cannot be expected to dedicate themselves to seeking out potential aid recipients; only when needy individuals present themselves are others obligated to supply their wants. However, once communication networks linking geographically distant communities are operating, persons who are bombarded daily by worldwide news cease to be ignorant of the plight of their far-flung fellows. Though personal contact with these impoverished strangers remains unfeasible for the most part, more advantaged individuals cannot conscionably exclude them from the claimant pool: they are right-holders, and their distress is broadcast globally.

A second difference between right-respecters in advanced economies and their counterparts in my elemental one concerns the provision of aid. Modern economic actors are highly specialized. Farmers, engineers, doctors, contractors, drug manufacturers, and the like have skills or supplies that they can donate to relief efforts, but many people can offer only funds. Furthermore, economic havoc would result if crises in rights respect were met through the temporary suspension of economic routine. Instead, experts must be hired, and they must purchase and dispense supplies and services to needy right-holders. Still, these professional respecters of the rights to benign treatment and satisfaction of basic needs must rely on others for financing.

The professionalization of responsibility for implementing rights to assistance spawns two types of distrust. Unlike the intimates of a small community, the reserve holdings of the countless individuals who might support aid programs are kept private. Not only is it unclear how much each person ought to contribute in view of the resources at her disposal, but it is also well known that many people are reluctant to contribute anything at all. Lacking any shared experience with the designated beneficiaries of organized rights respect, these individuals' empathic capacity is severely strained. In some instances, this understandable debilitation of moral bonds is further exacerbated by acceptance of an ideology that mistakenly rates property rights as stringent as, if not more stringent than, inalienable rights.[17]

Problems internal to the distributional scheme compound these difficulties. While communication and transportation facilities expand the scope of the individual's obligations to respect the rights to benign treatment and satisfaction of basic needs, the questionable practices of intermediaries may shrink it. Overpaid or corrupt administrators provide potential supporters with a convenient and legitimate excuse for declining to give in amounts sufficient to provide adequate care and to meet subsistence needs. Persons are obligated to secure the critical needs of other inalienable right-holders, not to enrich social service professionals. If well-intentioned donors cannot fulfill their obligations without incurring excessive overhead costs, they may justifiably neglect their obligations; that is, they may justifiably refuse to increase their contributions to cover extravagant middleman expenses since it is not their fault that their funds are diverted and misappropriated. Informal cooperative schemes, then, are apt to maldistribute the economic burdens and benefits of respecting the rights to benign treatment and satisfaction of basic needs under the moral circumstances that prevail in advanced industrial societies.

As in the case of enforcement of the rights to life and personal liberty and that aspect of the right to benign treatment which prohibits torture, implementation of the right to satisfaction of basic needs and the right to medical relief for acute pain is best achieved under the aegis of the state. If inalienable rights to assistance are to be respected, all right-holders who need and desire aid must be identified, the costs of providing this aid must be borne in proportion to right-respecters' ability to pay, and appropriate forms of aid must be delivered to the

Permissible Abridgment

rightful recipients. Without public agencies, satisfaction of these conditions is bound to be haphazard.

In societies in which many members are strangers, the potential for rights abuse multiplies exponentially. Whereas a member of a closely integrated community can conceal few of her resources, the anonymity of large nations may enable individuals to press fraudulent claims with impunity. Since individual right-respecters are not usually in a position to set reasonable standards of need and to separate the charlatans from the destitute, institutions equipped to perform these functions are indispensable. However, right-respecters are not vulnerable solely to the misrepresentations of opportunistic claimants; they may also be victimized by their affluent compatriots. If some individuals who have surplus resources give a deflated accounting of their possessions, others who have honestly reported their funds will appear to be responsible for a greater share of the expenses of rights respect than an accurate assessment would have assigned them. Again, anonymity may permit delinquency, and the only practicable and morally acceptable solution is state monitoring of available resources and state enforced levies. Not only are the institutions of the state geared to detect evaders of these duties, but also the answerability of public officials to their constituency restrains inordinate invasiveness as well as misuse of the information obtained in the process of rights implementation.

At this point, it might be objected that this deployment of state agencies in the service of the rights to benign treatment and satisfaction of basic needs authorizes an overly narrow view of the obligations these rights imply. Though the argument for state oversight to guarantee these rights may be sound, it gives credence to the idea of nationalistic rights respect, but many nation-states are currently too impoverished to implement these rights. In short, the call for state implementation seems to absolve the fortunate citizens of wealthy countries of responsibility for respecting the rights of persons who happen to live in poor ones.

This is a misapprehension. National borders do not

subdivide the community of moral agents unless they demarcate barriers to action.[18] In the primitive society I envisaged above, geographic boundaries are morally significant because communication and transportation facilities do not connect this community with others. Still, we can affirm that the members of this community would have broader responsibilities if their isolation ended and they had the wherewithal to assume these additional costs. Now, someone might retort that this characterization of their expanded duties is still vitiated by chauvinistic nationalism. For implicit in it is the assumption that this group should continue to care for its own members and afterward send extra resources to other communities. While it must be conceded that this conception of the duties correlative to the rights to benign treatment and satisfaction of basic needs is nation-centered, there are moral grounds for this view of the matter.

Identifying legitimate claims and collecting sufficient funds to honor them are only two of the obstacles to respecting rights to assistance. A final problem arises in the delivery process. Demands for assistance can be occasional or enduring depending on whether they stem from emergency conditions or from chronic ones. When deprivation is persistent, it is necessary to consider whether realizable changes in the economic infrastructure could solve the problem, that is, whether the economic system is structurally violating inalienable rights in the same way that a system of private rights enforcement would.[19] If so, rights respect requires long-run economic reform. But meanwhile, or if the hardship is unavoidable or temporary, relief must be provided. Funds must be converted into goods and services, and these must be distributed to right-holders with valid claims. At both levels—economic reform and aid dispensation—bad faith is possible, and both right-respecters and claimants must be protected from malfeasance.

A good reason underlying many bad reasons for regarding national boundaries as morally relevant to the provision of essential aid is that agencies within a state have maximal control over the delivery process. Committed to respecting the rights to benign treatment and satisfaction of basic needs, domestic officials can ensure that economic reforms are instituted and that no one siphons off funds or absconds with materiel. Of course, no human institution can bring about perfect implementation of these rights. But, in the absence of enforcement powers, no degree of determination and no quantity of resources can overcome a corrupt bureaucracy. The advantage of domestic programs is that they can be supervised effectively. Needless to say, where workable conduits for the delivery of aid are available abroad or mechanisms could easily be created, this justification for confining relief programs to domestic suffering is not germane and cannot properly be invoked. Nevertheless, occluding circumstances may justify concentrating on aiding proximate right-holders despite the universality of the inalienable rights to benign treatment and satisfaction of basic needs and their assertability against everyone.

8. The Difference Between Inalienable Rights and Obligations of Noninterference and Aid

Inalienable rights impose duties of respect on others. Since a person who has these rights is entitled not to be killed, subjugated, or subjected to acute gratuitous pain or severe deprivation, others have correlative obligations of noninterference and assistance. Furthermore, when abridging these rights proves necessary, duties to respect them are not canceled. Whether *in extremis* conditions or the commission of a crime occasions the infringement, inalienable rights persist in constraining other moral agents with respect to their procedures and actions.

Thus far, I have treated these diverse duties of respect as consequences of persons' inalienable rights; however, a moral system which drops inalienable rights but keeps the corresponding obligations might be proposed. Since this rightless moral system would confer the same benefits on moral agents as one containing inalienable rights, it could not be accused of withholding goods which these individuals need for moral agency. Thus, this innovation appears to satisfy the criteria of adequacy applicable to moral systems and raises the question of whether an obligation-based moral system could generate protection for moral agents extensionally equivalent to that provided by a moral system assigning them inalienable rights.

Human dignity and equality are often invoked to explain why moral systems cannot dispense with a set of universal basic rights.[20] Because rights give right-holders grounds for demanding that they be treated in ways specified by their rights and because a right-holder is entitled to press these claims against any moral agent, possession of rights enables a person to affirm his own worth and levels institutional hierarchical distinctions among people. While rights may be exceptionally well adapted to these purposes, it is possible that a moral system without rights could effectively sustain self-respect and instantiate moral equality.

In a community in which obligations were taken seriously, obligations would be neglected only as a result of oversights or conflicting, overriding obligations. Consequently, persons would consider it a favor to be reminded of forgotten duties—in this respect, they would all occupy the same moral plane—and the beneficiaries of others' unfulfilled duties could expect prompt remedial action or would be assured that inaction was justified. Thus, they would respect one another reciprocally. Admittedly, a realistic view of human fallibility and prejudice argues for recognizing a distinct moral title to protest others' laxity or meanness. Still, among conscientious individuals the elimination of rights would not inevitably undermine personal dignity or moral equality.

Yet, a problem remains about whether a set of obligations could capture the same content as the set of inalienable rights without implicitly admitting these rights.[21] An agent might derive his obligations from any of an assortment of ultimate principles, including such diverse ones as Mill's principle of utility, Kant's categorical imperative, and Ayn Rand's rational selfishness. In practice, these principles might over an extended

Permissible Abridgment 177

period of time create pockets of security coinciding with the protection afforded by inalienable rights for the same individuals who would possess inalienable rights if these rights were to be introduced into the moral universe. Since the beneficiaries of these obligations would enjoy the same area of security that inalienable rights define, they would have no difficulty maintaining moral relations. This suggests that what is essential to moral agency is the security I have formulated in terms of inalienable rights, not the inalienable rights themselves. However, examination of the analogue of an infringement of an inalienable right reveals that obligations do not establish identical protection for individuals.

As noted above, it can be permissible to infringe a person's inalienable rights. Similarly, any criterion for ascertaining duties would occasionally allow or dictate an invasion of someone's pocket of security. How would this situation differ from an infringement of an inalienable right? The most prominent discrepancy is that there could be an obligation to invade someone's de facto pocket of security, whereas infringing an inalienable right cannot be morally required. An obligation-based pocket of security is merely a fortunate accident since it has no status independent of the ground of obligation that shapes its contours. Consequently, practical prescriptions can change radically in response to new conditions, and the pocket may contract or vanish altogether. This malleability affects the structure of moral intercourse when actions equivalent to inalienable rights infringements are appropriate.

Only when two or more courses of conduct satisfy a criterion of obligation to the same degree or no course of conduct satisfies the criterion of obligation in the least does an obligation-based moral system issue permissions. In all other situations, including ones in which individuals may sacrifice the objects of inalienable rights or these goods may be taken from them, these moral systems prescribe. An agent's failure to carry out these prescriptions is culpable.

Inalienable rights address these situations more tentatively. They allow right-holders to sacrifice the objects of these rights, and they recognize the superlative moral merit of doing so altruistically. Thus, a moral system founded on inalienable rights rewards spontaneous self-sacrifice undertaken to contend with fearsome crises. Such moral systems may concede that various desiderata would be better served if one person were to sacrifice himself rather than another, but they do not appraise the expendability of candidates in order to prescribe their sacrifice seriatim. Inalienable rights prize the personal virtues of moral agents, their willingness to deny their own interests to the advantage of others', over the values that might be achieved through tighter moral control. Criteria of obligation reverse this ranking. They dictate a solution, and, though their prescriptions can demand great fortitude or humility, discharging the duties they specify cannot be supererogatory.

Now, it might be urged that moral systems deriving from a standard of obligation would not necessarily prescribe invasions of the pockets of security corresponding to inalienable rights. Like rights-based moral systems, obligation-based ones could confine themselves to permitting analogues of infringements. However, it is out of the question that any teleological system could be committed to principled indifference regarding who will live, act autonomously, and be free of pain and deprivation. Whatever the posited goal, sometimes its attainment will be differentially affected by choices between conflicting inalienable rights since right-holders are the agents of the goal's realization but they are not all capable of contributing equally to its realization. In that event, the moral system will be obliged to prescribe the infringement least detrimental to the goal. Furthermore, it is hard to see how a deontological system which excludes rules constitutive of inalienable rights could avoid prescribing infringements. If the moral system's precepts forbidding aggression and deprivation were inflexible, the code would break down whenever these duties came into conflict. But to avoid this excessive rigidity, deontological systems must allow for the possibility of mandatory killing, subjugation, torture, and severe deprivation. If ever the system's body of regulations

Permissible Abridgment

would be better implemented by one infringement rather than any available alternative, the system would be compelled to prescribe the former course. Only if a deontological system's rules covertly formulate inalienable rights is it certain that the moral system will refrain from prescribing infringements.

Unlike inalienable rights which reflect the qualifications of the individuals who possess them, obligations manifest only the standards from which they are derived. As a result, *in extremis* situations sharply differentiate these types of moral systems. Whereas rights-based conduct guides can permit only voluntary self-sacrifice or a lottery to decide the futures of equally qualified right-holders, criteria of obligation can discriminate among these individuals and can impose duties orchestrating their handling of the crisis. Moreover, these root differences do not appear exclusively in farfetched circumstances. In the everyday matter of enforcement, rights-based and obligation-based moral systems may disagree.

Right-holders are entitled to assert their inalienable rights, that is, to establish preemptive defenses and to exact recognition of their victimization if their rights are violated, but these individuals are not capable of enforcing their own rights while respecting the rights of others. Since state enforcement solves this dilemma, inalienable rights reflexively justify public enforcement. Where conferral of comparable protections depends on a criterion of obligation, however, enforcement also hinges on this standard. Of course, many ultimate moral objectives and sets of moral rules would be well served by state enforcement of protections equivalent to inalienable rights. Still, obligation-based moral systems do not rule out transferring enforcement resources to other rights—for example, utility estimates could warrant enforcing the property rights of a large affluent class instead of a small impoverished class's rights to satisfaction of basic needs—or withdrawing enforcement from rights altogether—for example, a principle of self-perfection could substitute voluntary charity for enforcement of the right to satisfaction of basic needs. Not only do inalienable rights provide more substantial protections for right-holders than obligations do over a full range of cases, but they also provide a more reliable form of security than a system of obligations would because inalienable rights carry with them a justification for routine public enforcement.

9. The Ineliminability of Inalienable Rights

In order to create an obligation-based moral system that provides the same security as inalienable rights, it would be necessary to devise a criterion of obligation which generates a set of obligations which requires the same forbearance and aid as inalienable rights afford and which are owed equally and only to moral agents. But it is doubtful that this task can be accomplished without echoing the rationale for inalienable rights.

One way to approach this project is through the fiat of an authority. Obligation fulfillment can be defined as carrying out a deity's will, and this god can be represented as willing that persons should refrain from killing, subjugating, tormenting, and depriving one another. Apart from the dubiety of religious dogma, the trouble with this strategy is that the obligations the authority promulgates would be owed to the authority, not to the proximate beneficiaries.[22] Though a divine authority can command equal consideration within the class of moral agents, reverence for this authority, as opposed to other persons' entitlements, would elicit compliance with this imperative.

To repair to the secular perspective, however, is to forgo the mysteries of divine pronouncements to explain why the obligations usually associated with inalienable rights are owed equally to all moral agents. We have seen that familiar teleological and deontological grounds of obligation are capable of disrupting the equality of these obligations. How could this capacity be counteracted? Two adjustments suggest themselves. Either these moral systems must be weakened, or they must be supplemented.

If the controlling value of a teleological system were so elemental that all moral agents would be equally adept at promoting it, or if the rules of a deontological system were so elastic that any action involving a moral agent's life, liberty, benign treatment, or access to basic necessities would equally satisfy them, these moral systems would have no reason to prescribe unequal treatment of moral agents in regard to their fundamental interests. Unfortunately, it is not clear that these systems would constrain conduct sufficiently to count as moral systems. A teleological moral system must pursue some value (or set of values) that is not only worth achieving but possible not to achieve. If it defined moral conduct as action promoting a goal that will inevitably be achieved, no action would be immoral. Likewise, a deontological moral system must exact conformity with rules which can be abrogated. But a moral system hearkening to a goal which no one can advance any better than anyone else or devoted to a set of rules that do not differentiate among persons' diverse characters and plans would prescribe trivial restrictions, at most.

In order to weaken teleological and deontological obligation-based moral systems enough to block their prescribing differential obligations concerning life, personal liberty, benign treatment, and satisfaction of basic needs, they must be sapped of their normative force. The only remaining way to check their discriminating principles so as to replicate the substance of inalienable rights is to graft onto them a principle to supersede the former when the objects of inalienable rights are at stake. This powerful addendum would declare that moral agents in virtue of their sharing some morally significant property (or properties) ought to be treated equally with respect to life, personal liberty, benign treatment, and satisfaction of basic needs. In light of the fact that the moral systems to which this principle is to be appended are capable of generating prescriptions incompatible with it, the justification for this principle must be sought outside these moral systems. It must furnish qualifications which these moral systems overlook but which warrant the requisite egalitarianism. It would come as no surprise if this superordinate principle implicitly invoked the rationale for inalienable rights to justify the constraints it imposes on conflicting moral precepts.

The suggestion that a set of obligations replace inalienable rights is empty. Though it is possible to reformulate the content of inalienable rights as an elaborate set of prima facie obligations which secure assorted benefits for all persons and establish opportunities for these persons to voice their grievances, this contrivance is inextricable from inalienable rights. The principles of moral systems that exclude inalienable rights do not indirectly capture the content of these rights, and this content cannot be injected into these moral systems unless the principles that justify inalienable rights are imported into them, too.

Because many moral systems that deny inalienable rights approximate the moral force of these rights in a broad selection of cases, they are able to sustain their adherents' moral agency for the most part. However, where the prescriptions of these systems diverge from those inalienable rights would generate, they make excessive demands on persons and yet expect these individuals to adapt to these privations in the line of duty. Either these moral systems must apply only to persons who find the burden of moral guilt worse than any other form of suffering, or they must hasten to deploy force to police compliance with their dicta. In contrast, moral systems which recognize inalienable rights proffer a more substantial combination of moral and egoistic incentives to extend moral interaction to the limits of their adherents' endurance when infringements loom before them. These moral systems set sacrifices of the objects of inalienable rights apart from commonplace moral matters, esteeming them as supererogatory gestures and encouraging the hesitant through compensatory considerations. Though circumstances could conceivably be so terrible and prospective adherents so venal that no moral system could take credit if utter calamity were averted, moral systems that respect inalienable rights forge a network of assurances among moral agents that prevents premature curtailment of moral interaction.

7

Contract Theory and Inalienable Rights

The account of inalienable rights complete, it is now possible to reflect on the method by which it was obtained and to juxtapose that method with social contract doctrine. Though major contract theories differ sharply in crucial respects, they share an assumption that natural rights are fundamental to political philosophy and a conjecture that a prescription for political society can be articulated through the hypothetical device of the social contract. The theory of inalienable rights I have advanced is by no means as comprehensive as the classical theories of Hobbes, Locke, and Rousseau, nor as the recent work of John Rawls. I have nowhere pretended that a theory of inalienable rights suffices to found a complete social ideal. Nevertheless, the inalienable rights recommended above would hang in theoretical limbo if they were not finally situated in this broad philosophical tradition.

1. Defending Natural Rights

Contract doctrines are often criticized for relying on a set of natural rights which have been defended unpersuasively, if at all. Locke's arguments for the rights to life, liberty, and property, for example, and Rousseau's discussion of inalienable liberty are suggestive but cursory. Yet, both of these philosophers unabashedly rest revolutionary political doctrines on these shaky foundations. The first and primary aim of a theory of inalienable rights is to discredit the contention that the foundations of political philosophy are necessarily ramshackle. To that end I have derived a set of inalienable rights from three kinds of premises: a conceptual analysis of inalienable rights, a pair of criteria of adequacy for moral systems, and key facts about human vulnerability and self-control.

To set forth conditions of adequacy for moral systems is to fix conditions of the possibility of responsibility for compliance with moral dicta and, conversely, of the possibility of culpability for noncompliance. Persons may diligently follow a moral system that fails to meet these criteria, and under some conditions they may be absolved of blame for carrying out prescriptions that no adequate moral system could generate. But no one can justifiably be condemned for defying an unsatisfactory moral system's imperatives unless the same prescriptions could have been obtained from an adequate moral system of which he should have been cognizant.

Moral systems, we have seen, must be neither self-defeating—they must not prescribe conduct bringing moral interaction to a halt—nor self-rescinding—they must not permit conduct that engenders moral relations inimical to moral interaction. Whereas a self-defeating moral system's capacity to prescribe the demise of moral relations requires persons to uphold incomprehensible, if not wicked, moral imperatives, a self-rescinding moral system prevents persons from maintaining intelligible social relations unless they are prepared to suffer extreme hardship or serious injury. Together, these negative criteria of adequacy set limits on the extent to which morality can stretch the credulity of or compromise the interests of moral agents. To exact passivity in the face of terrible threats or apocalyptic destruction is to release moral agents from their duties.

The alternative to this solicitous view of human agency is one which requires persons to accept the guidance of a religious or secular authority when reason fails, and which places persons completely at the disposal of moral directives. On this sterner view, moral systems may posit any end and must implant in individuals those beliefs and attitudes needed to serve whatever ends these moral systems aver. In contrast, my criteria of adequacy presuppose that persons are endowed with certain abilities and vulnerabilities—abilities to reason and control conduct, and vulnerabilities to aggression and deprivation—and that, if persons can be molded to suppress or distort these abilities and interests, doing so perverts their nature. Unlike moral systems predicated on a concept of autonomous responsibility, moral systems espousing a responsibility of subservience withhold dignity from their adherents and imperil their hold on these individuals.

Inalienable rights cannot be renounced conscientiously because they entitle persons to goods which it cannot be obligatory to sacrifice and which it is supererogatory, if appropriate, to sacrifice altruistically. Moreover, they cannot be renounced by fiat because the liberties thus created are antithetical to moral relations. In order not to be self-defeating or self-rescinding, moral systems must refrain both from obligating their adherents to relinquish goods which they need to act as moral agents and from permitting their adherents to compete for these goods on a quotidian basis. It follows that moral systems must recognize inalienable rights to those goods persons need to conduct themselves morally. Which goods these are depends on the empirically ascertainable vulnerabilities of prospective moral agents, and, I have argued, life, personal liberty, benign treatment, and satisfaction of basic needs are among them.

Both Locke and Rousseau advert directly to human nature to account for natural rights. Persons, Locke contends, are free and equal creations of God and therefore ought not to be killed, enslaved, or deprived of their property. Though Rousseau's view of humanity is much like Locke's (the admixture of natural pity is not foreign to Locke), his interpretation of the liberty and property rights vested in persons departs radically from Locke's. This disparity in their conclusions is hardly surprising in light of the sparseness of their premises. Lacking both an analysis of natural rights and a specification of the larger moral system that is to host these rights, Locke's and Rousseau's claims about rights are conjectures delivered without the benefit of articulated conceptual supports.

Of the major classical contract theorists, Hobbes stands alone in providing an account of morality that locates his ideas about fundamental rights. Hobbes holds that adherence to moral rules ensures peace, which is a universal goal inasmuch as it presages personal survival. Though this analysis of morality is an impoverished one (surely some sets of rules capable of guaranteeing peace would not count as adequate moral systems), it is important to note that the inalienable rights Hobbes enunciates are fully intelligible within the theoretical context he supplies. Persons must retain liberties to resist assault and to withhold self-incriminating information since relinquishing these would conflict with the individual's purpose in committing himself to a moral system, namely, self-preservation, and thus with the overarching purpose of moral systems, namely, peace. Whereas Locke and Rousseau dodge the very question that would illuminate the backgrounds of their respective rights positions, Hobbes plunges into the philosophical thicket. Though his overly simplistic account of morality leads him to propound a deficient set of natural rights, his theory of inalienable rights is formally complete.

In a similar vein, I might be accused of relying on too narrow an account of morality for my theory of inalienable rights. Specifically, this theory depends on viewing moral systems as sets of principles regulating the interaction of autonomous agents. Yet, moral systems might instead be viewed as governing the collaboration amongst individuals on a social end or as directing individuals toward the attainment of personal perfection. Why embrace a Kantian conception of morality to the exclusion of these other possibilities?

To accept the theory of inalienable rights I have proffered is to adopt a Kantian conception of morality only in a limited sphere. Any moral system must account for the possibility of moral responsibility in a satisfactory way. A notable flaw in Rousseau's collectivist approach to morality and moral responsibility is that the agent, when "forced to be free," ceases to be the locus of responsibility. The general will or, at any rate, the community's interpretation of it supplants the individual and appropriates his role as moral contributor to a social objective. Likewise, theories of self-perfection must provide a context in which the individual's responsibility for realizing the envisaged ideal is assured. I would urge that a plausible background account of some necessary conditions for moral responsibility can be obtained using a Kantian model of morality that generates inalienable rights. Nevertheless, it remains possible to build various kinds of teleological or collectivist moralities upon a foundation of inalienable rights. Since these rights merely establish the moral setting in which any code of conduct can claim to be an adequate moral one, they constrain the operation of other principles but do not ordain the form these principles must take.

Like Hobbes, John Rawls has attempted a comprehensive exposition of the conceptual underpinnings of political principles, as well as personal and international morality. To accomplish this remarkable feat, Rawls formulates conditions of adequacy for this triad of normative conduct codes. Roughly, he maintains that those principles chosen in the original position (and its variations)—a hypothetical decision situation in which persons know enough about themselves and their societies to be able to choose principles (or a constitution or laws) but not enough about themselves to be able to skew their choices to promote their individual interests—constitute an adequate normative action guide. In his more recent work Rawls explicitly rejects the proposition that there must be a unique correct description of the original position.[1] Though he contends that only one set of principles can be chosen by the parties to the original position under a given description, his theory is indeterminate inasmuch as he allows that the ideals of the person prevalent in diverse cultures and epochs can be embodied in correspondingly divergent accounts of the original position to yield an assortment of normative programs. Rawls does not, however, speculate as to whether any features are common to all admissible treatments of the original position, features that might guarantee a universal, though perhaps small, body of normative doctrine.

In setting out full conditions of adequacy for prescriptive guides to state and individual conduct, Hobbes and Rawls construct the conceptual machinery for generating complete moral and political theories. More modestly, the theory of inalienable rights elaborated in this book defends and invokes only two necessary conditions for an adequate moral system from which four inalienable rights (and a complementary one for children) and the state's powers to enforce them are derived. Yet, if no adequate moral system can be self-defeating or self-rescinding, and if the central facts about human vulnerability and self-control are stable, and if it follows that persons are endowed with inalienable rights to life, personal liberty, benign treatment, and satisfaction of basic needs, these rights must be enshrined in all adequate moral systems. Their directives are definitive.

2. Political Ideals

Contract theory, as traditionally understood, took its task to be the justification of a political order on the basis of a state of nature—a conception of prepolitical human existence—coupled with a social contract—an analysis of the terms upon which political relations ought to be founded. Treatments of the state of nature differ widely. Hobbes produces his infamous state of war in which each individual is every other's enemy and life is commensurately wretched; Locke envisages a relatively placid and prosperous state of nature in which persons discover morality through reason and are thereby able to avoid the strife Hobbes thinks inevitable; Rousseau offers a vision of amoral, entirely independent individuals who form premoral associations as a result of filial dependency and familial affection. Striking as these contrasts are, these theories nevertheless converge in regard to the underlying assumption that persons are naturally free. Again, they disagree about the proper analysis of natural freedom—many of the discrepancies in their accounts of the state of nature can be traced to this fundamental controversy—yet they concur in thinking that it poses an obstacle to government. Since persons are naturally free, they cannot be legitimately ruled unless they give their consent to an artificial authority. Hence, a social contract must be concluded.

Now, it might be observed that the inhabitants of the state of nature could choose to remain in this anarchical condition rather than submit to government. Most notably in Rousseau's work, a strain of nostalgia for prepolitical bliss occasionally surfaces. However, none of these states of nature is conceived in such a way that declining to organize politically is a tenable option. Hobbes' state of nature is intolerable and must give way to the state; Locke's moral relations are hobbled by uncertainty without state enforcement of natural rights; Rousseau's state of nature is bound to degenerate initially into philistine civilization but is populated by individuals whose most exalted capability, their potential for moral interaction, will be stunted unless they embrace political relations. In thus maintaining that persons must ally themselves to form states, these authors imply that natural liberty is properly, if not inevitably, limited by legitimate political authority. If this is so, the consent of the governed is not necessary to extinguish natural liberty. And despite the salience these theorists accord the idea of consent, the social contract is best viewed as a particularly dramatic expository device.

What purpose, then, is served by detailing a state of nature? For different reasons, Hobbes and Rousseau hold that moral interaction is critical to human existence. The virtue of contract theories like these two that begin with an amoral state of nature is that they vividly convey their authors' views about why compliance with a moral system is good. The disadvantage of these theories is that they tend to obscure the conceptual ties between adherence to adequate moral systems and the state. Hobbes vaults over this difficulty by appealing to his egoistic doctrines. Only the coercive power of the state, Hobbes warns, can tame rampant egoism. But in Rousseau this link is tenuous. Apart from the historical contingency of increasingly populous and geographically dispersed societies which can only be unified by political institutions, it never becomes clear why Rousseau believes the state to be necessary for full development of the individual's moral capability. In contrast, Locke, who starts from a state of nature replete with moral principles, occupies a vantage point from which he can discern that private enforcement of natural rights may precipitate social upheaval. Contract theories premised on states of nature in which persons interact morally are singularly adapted to display the reciprocity binding the moral and political realms: on the one side, the constraints morality imposes on politics and, on the other side, the support political institutions lend to moral communities.

That there ought to be political institutions is an inescapable conclusion once inalienable rights have been shown to be necessary contents of adequate moral systems. Persons possessing inalienable rights are at liberty to assert their rights. Rights assertion spans laying claim to benefits, opposing possible violations, resisting attempted violations, and demanding acknowledgment of victimization in the aftermath of violations. But unless a properly constituted public authority defines the entitlements conferred by these rights and secures respect for them, rights assertion becomes fraught with distrust and irresolvable conflict. State mediation enables persons to assert their rights because it ensures that rights assertion does not conceal rights violation. Consequently, to reject political authority is to induce degenerate moral interaction and, possibly, to destroy the infrastructure of moral interaction altogether.

Locke's conception of a moral community unencumbered by political authority is misleading to the extent that it is portrayed as a stable forum for moral interaction and as a viable alternative to a moral-political complex. However, its strength

Contract Theory

lies in its exposition of the restrictions under which government must operate. The social contract, as Locke interprets it, is constrained by the natural rights persons possess. Since they cannot relinquish these rights and since private enforcement of them jeopardizes moral relations, persons must create a state to guarantee their rights and cannot create a state that voids them. Although Rousseau's thinking on this matter is comparatively convoluted, he, too, invokes a fundamental moral endowment, the inalienable liberty of the individual, to formulate the social contract and thus to commend a political schema. On his theory, however, individual rights mainly shape political institutions rather than restricting the content of legislation.

The inalienable rights to life, personal liberty, benign treatment, and satisfaction of basic needs exert a pull on the state similar to that of Locke's natural rights. These rights, we have seen, must be enforced by a public authority which is debarred from abrogating this function. But whereas Locke is sometimes interpreted as holding that the state ought to undertake no projects beyond rights enforcement, the theory of inalienable rights I propose does not demarcate the range of the state's rightful powers. There may be other rights, such as democratic political rights, that the state ought to implement, and social goods, such as public works, that the state ought to provide. Since these additional rights and benefits may be wholly independent of inalienable rights, it remains to be shown either that public authority is confined to enforcing these rights or that justice mandates more extensive state powers.

Intuitively, respect for inalienable rights seems not to suffice for justice. A regime that secures the bare survival of its citizenry while disproportionately enriching itself may respect inalienable rights but is not just. Similarly, a benign dictatorship does not qualify as just despite its respect for inalienable rights. No doubt, countless forms of exploitation and repression are not ruled out by inalienable rights though these iniquities are incompatible with justice. Still, it is arguable that respect for inalienable rights constitutes a threshold condition for realization of a just society. Rawls, for example, maintains that his special conception of justice—two principles requiring maximum equal liberties, fair equality of opportunity, and a social and economic system with power and wealth differentials designed to improve the expectations of the least advantaged—can only come into play at levels of affluence that obviate forced labor and that enable basic needs to be met.[2] More generally and without endorsing the details of Rawls' account of justice, it is evident that the value of justice cannot be instantiated unless mutual consideration and moral responsibility are possible. For this, inalienable rights must be respected.

3. Individualism

Classical contract theory's methodological commitment to constructing a society composed of primordially self-sufficient persons has indelibly branded this mode of argument with the contentions that the state is established to provide a safe setting for the pursuit of self-interest and that its failure to do so justifies the individual's withdrawal. Because natural rights made their historical debut and figure prominently in contract theories that by no means disavow these claims, this substantive individualism bordering on egoism has gradually come to be linked with natural rights.[3] Yet, it is not at all clear that there is any necessary connection between natural rights and individualism, except as found in the truism that individuals possess these rights.

States of nature that attribute some form of liberty to asocial persons conjure up an image of lone individuals who have no use for their freedom other than to promote their own interests. Hobbes exacerbates the divisive consequences of this freedom by positing an egoistic motivational structure that drives free individuals; however, Rousseau dispatches this notion by stressing the independence of these individuals and their natural aversion to witnessing others' suffering. Leaning less heavily on speculation about human instinct, Locke takes an ethical approach. Persons, on his view, have natural rights which they are free to exercise for their own betterment, but they are morally obligated to aid others if their own survival is not threatened. Despite the reputation for virulent individualism Locke's views about property rights have earned him in some quarters, his individualism is tempered by the assumption that persons are naturally subject to moral principles.

Nevertheless, focusing on Locke's individualism is not entirely unwarranted. He affirms that God entrusts persons with their own preservation and grants them natural rights in order that they may fulfill this divine mission. However, in addition to affording persons the moral latitude they need to preserve themselves, natural rights enable persons to discharge other sacred trusts like improving on the productivity of nature through work and thrift and capital formation. This latter enterprise transmutes self-preservation into self-aggrandizement. Because one of the natural rights Locke identifies as instruments for survival, namely, the right to property, is amenable to deployment in the service of personal economic gain, his benign expectation that individuals should take care of themselves and should help the needy when possible assumes a sinister mercenary aspect.

Part of the trouble is that Locke derives natural rights from the wrong source. Since he defends natural rights as props to survival, right-holders can point out that grave misfortunes can unexpectedly reduce vast wealth to meager proportions, and they can insist that these familiar hazards justify their proclivity for precautionary accumulation. But once it is evident that inalienable rights are founded on criteria of adequacy for moral systems which do not entail a duty of self-preservation, this excuse for diverting natural rights to advance selfish aims ceases to be available. Moreover, Locke's list of natural rights is incorrect. There is no inalienable right to property. There is only the inalienable right to satisfaction of basic needs. Rights to acquire property and to use it may be defended as means of respecting the right to satisfaction of basic needs. But if anyone is incapable of exercising property rights to meet his basic needs, supplemental measures which may intrude on others' property rights must be instituted to secure respect for this individual's subsistence rights. Beyond this, it is an open question what configuration of property rights moral argument and pragmatic exigencies will sustain.

Economic individualism has no intrinsic connection to natural rights. Still, political individualism and natural rights might be inextricable. The thesis of political individualism can assert either that, to be legitimate, governments must obtain the consent of each citizen, or that government disregard for inalienable rights justifies persons in withdrawing allegiance from the state. We have seen that the first of these positions is incoherent. The second, however, is deeply entrenched in the natural rights tradition. Hobbes, of course, contends that the social contract is absolutely binding, in other words, that rebellion is never permissible. However, since Hobbes' social contract leaves the individual with no rights that the government is obliged to protect, his denial that government dereliction justifies revolt is to be expected. Contrariwise, both Rousseau and Locke authorize individuals to emigrate from or to rebel against despotic government. These two theories typify the natural rights-based approach to the problem of political legitimacy.

Whatever else they do, legitimate governments enforce every person's inalienable rights impartially and fairly. Still, countless governments have violated inalienable rights, sometimes willfully by killing, incarcerating, and torturing real or imagined enemies and sometimes negligently by maintaining a lax judicial system. In either case, state enforcement duplicates the problem of private enforcement. Right-holders are beset by the possibility of rights violations but lack a trustworthy remedy. A despotic government does not enforce its constitutents' rights or enforces them only selectively. Thus, it fails to act conscientiously as the agent of all right-holders who have reason to assert their rights. Rights assertion, then, must revert to right-holders who can direct their claims against the state in self-defense. As Locke and Rousseau put it, persons are in a state of nature with respect to the government in power and may take necessary steps to end this predicament. Just as private enforcement fatally infects moral communities, vicious or incompetent public enforcement deprives persons of the security upon which moral interaction thrives.

Inalienable rights imply political individualism inasmuch as government victimization of right-holders authorizes these individuals to elude these practices by emigrating or to marshal their own defenses and eliminate the cause of their mistreatment.[4] However, the expression 'political individualism' is something of a misnomer. Oppressed individuals can, of course, emigrate singly; however, each must enter some other political association. Since the option of resigning membership in all human societies is illusory, the individualism of emigration is confined to the right-holder's decision to depart and her choice of a destination. Emigration extricates a person from one set of social bonds only to enmesh her in another.

Revolution also requires cooperation. Whereas a wronged individual's valiant attack on a tyrannical regime is bound to prove futile and probably disastrous for the right-holder, a victim of state persecution who escapes and hides changes nothing. Only concerted action against an illegitimate state holds any promise of success. Furthermore, though revolutionary groups must remain clandestine during their preparations for revolt, they can sustain moral interaction among their members. They function as paragovernments enforcing their members' rights and upholding their common political ideals. In contrast, the solitary fugitive lives anonymously in a moral vacuum penetrated, if at all, by others' pity and by her gratitude to persons who shelter her. Furthermore, unless she finds an underground of victims and their sympathizers who can conceal her and supply her needs, her withdrawal makes her a renegade, dangerous to innocent individuals and destitute of company. Both for tactical reasons and for moral ones, political individualism must yield to collective rebellion or organized internal exile. Otherwise, the prerogatives redounding to individual right-holders would be powerless to maintain provisional private respect for inalienable rights or to restore public enforcement of them.

Inalienable rights undeniably serve the interests of individuals. When enforced, they provide a fundamental measure of security; when violated, they provide a justification for mounting a strenuous defense. Nevertheless, there is no basis for accusing inalienable rights of promoting pernicious individualism. These rights do not afford individuals seductive opportunities to profit to others' detriment, and they do not authorize disgruntled right-holders to renounce their political obligations for disreputably selfish reasons. Inalienable rights embody the distinctness of individuals inasmuch as there are goods which persons can only enjoy separately and some of these are objects of inalienable rights. However, it is a mistake to regard inalienable rights as capturing the essential independence of persons. Persons have inalienable rights not because they are capable of surviving alone in a state of nature but because they are capable of engaging in moral interaction with others. Moreover, in securing only critical state and private assistance for right-holders, these rights raise minimal barriers to state and private interference in right-holders' lives. Inalienable rights thus ensure the individual's ability to conduct himself morally but do not so fill moral space as to prejudge what principles should govern a good society.

Because inalienable rights are anchored in the inherently social idea of an agent participating in a moral community, they are not susceptible to the complaint that they elevate the lowest human impulses while suppressing noble aspiration. A moral community is a society in which individuals who are capable of moral agency but vulnerable to morally incapacitating injuries regulate themselves according to a moral system that is sensitive to their highest purposes along with their fundamental needs. Through the instrument of the inalienable right, adequate moral systems respond to those crucial human needs which must be met if persons are to be held morally responsible, while allowing individuals to embrace diverse personal ideals. In virtue of this grounding in the activity of moral interaction, the inalienable rights to life, personal liberty, benign treatment, and satisfaction of basic needs both unite persons and revere them as individuals.

Notes

1. The Problem Of Natural Rights

1. Sometimes inalienable rights are defined as ones that can neither be lost by those who possess them nor justifiably abridged by those who are called upon to respect them. This definition collapses two separate sets of issues. Consequently, I have reserved the term 'inalienable' for rights that cannot be lost and will use the term 'absolute' for rights that can never be abridged justifiably.

2. See Judith Jarvis Thomson's observations in this regard in "Some Ruminations on Rights," pp. 54–56.

3. Seminal papers touching on the question of rights possession include the following: Frankena's "The Concept of Universal Human Rights," pp. 196–198; Melden's "The Play of Rights," pp. 490–493; Thomson's "Rights and Compensation," p. 3–15; Lyons' "Utility as a Possible Ground of Rights," pp. 20–22; and Joel Feinberg's "The Nature and Value of Rights," pp. 243–257.

4. Because different rights are regarded as starting with differential base stringencies and because each right's stringency varies with circumstances, the idea of a reason sufficiently compelling to override a right resists general characterization. Nevertheless it is clear that stronger reasons must be given for an action that is ordinarily barred by someone's right than would need to be given for the same action in the absence of anyone's right.

5. Ronald Dworkin characterizes the normative force of rights in a similar way (*Taking Rights Seriously*, pp. 169–170).

6. A widely known case of nonassertion of a right being interpreted as tacit consent to abridgment concerns right-of-way in property law. If a property owner permits

a person to cross his land for ten years (the cutoff point varies with state law) without demurral, the erstwhile trespasser acquires a right to use his accustomed path.

7. If there are any inalienable mandatory rights—that is, rights to goods which the right-holder has no right to refuse—this mode of exercising the right would be confined to accepting the object of the right should it be offered.

8. Notice that it is not helpful to declare that the ultimate principle must dictate which principle of adjudication to deploy. For persons may disagree about which procedural principle their absolute principle selects in the same way that they disagree about its substantive requirements. In that case, either they must use secondary moral considerations to pick a procedure, or one of them must simply defer to the other. I assume that no unambiguous decision-procedure could capture morality and could serve as the ultimate principle.

9. It should be noted that moral considerations other than rights could negate the proximate normative consequences of a person's renunciation of a right. If others have duties independent of those imposed by the person's right that invariably forbid conduct violative of the right, these duties would remain in force despite the right-holder's renunciation, and the renunciation would be practically vacuous. If this moral constellation obtained, however, it would follow that the right in question was superfluous. Thus, in dealing with the problem of renunciation, it is necessary to assume that renunciation could release others from their obligations to the right-holder in at least some circumstances and, accordingly, that the former right-holder is liable to new harms. For more detailed treatments of the import of renunciation and the differences between rights-based duties and duties stemming from other sources, see chapter 2, section 1 and chapter 6, sections 8 and 9.

10. On one interpretation, Hobbes' contention that inalienable rights are rights that cannot be advantageously traded is a psychological account (*Leviathan*, ch. 14). Stuart Brown's views regarding inalienable rights are similar ("Inalienable Rights," pp. 192–211).

11. Locke's treatment of natural rights is the prototype of accounts based on the concept of a person. He holds that persons have these rights because of the way God created them (*The Second Treatise of Government*, sec. 6). Both Herbert Morris ("Persons and Punishment," pp. 111–134) and Robert Nozick (*Anarchy, State, and Utopia*, pp. 28–51) follow Locke's approach, though they do not rely on religious beliefs.

12. T. H. Green offers an account of inalienable rights derived from a social ideal (*Lectures*, secs. 7 and 9). W.T. Blackstone's approach, ("Equality and Human Rights," pp. 616–639), and Martin Golding's ("Towards a Theory of Human Rights," pp. 521–549) resemble Green's.

13. The criteria of adequacy which I rely on to develop an account of inalienable rights are discussed in chapter 2, section 3 and in chapter 4, section 1. Alan Gewirth's defense of rights to freedom and well-being in terms of the concept of an agent and a principle of consistency employs a method similar to the one I propose (*Reason and Morality*, pp. 63–103).

14. For further discussion of the distinction between absolute rights and inalienable rights, see chapter 1, section 2.

15. Adina Schwartz's recent argument urging that entrepreneurial risk-takers cannot be persuaded of Rawls' principles of justice and that security-seekers cannot be persuaded of Nozick's entitlement theory might be construed as distinguishing moral systems appropriate to different moral spheres ("Against Universality," pp. 127–143). It

would, however, be a mistake to do so. Rawls and Nozick address the same agents and contend with the same problems; they differ about how these individuals ought to handle their problems, or, as Rawls would put it, they share a concept of justice but do not have the same conception. That this is the extent of their disagreement is indicated by the fact that Rawls offers arguments aimed at persuading Nozick's constituency that they should accept his two principles, while Nozick tries to entice Rawls' constituency by pointing out that free social experimentation will allow them to establish communities answering to their needs. In addition, their views about the individuals who can be just and who are owed justice are remarkably similar. There is little to distinguish Rawls' "moral person" who is capable of conceiving a rational plan of life which he thinks worth pursuing and who is capable of having a sense of justice from Nozick's individual who is capable of living a "meaningful life" (A *Theory of Justice*, pp. 5 and 505, and *Anarchy, State and Utopia*, pp. 49–50).

2. A Contribution of Inalienable Rights to the Adequacy of Moral Systems

1. See chapter 1, section 3 for treatment of the relation between renunciation, on the one hand, and conditional waiver, transfer, forfeiture, and revocation, on the other.

2. For an argument against absolute obligations, see chapter 1, section 3.

3. Wesley Newcomb Hohfeld distinguishes rights from liberties, noting that liberties (or privileges) "designate the mere negation of duty" whereas we "are accustomed to thinking of 'duty' as the invariable correlative" of rights (or claims) (*Fundamental Legal Conceptions*, pp. 38 and 44). In other words, if a person has a right to x, others are obligated not to interfere in his enjoyment of x or his doing x, and they may be obligated to supply x; however, if a person has a liberty with respect to x, he has no duty to do or not to do x or no duty to enjoy or refrain from enjoying x.

4. See chapter 1, section 2 for detailed treatment of these prerogatives.

5. "Six Make Their Way in the World," Francis P. Magoun, Jr., and Alexander H. Krappe, trans., *The Grimms' German Folk Tales* (Carbondale: Southern Illinois University Press, 1960).

6. In suggesting that some actions are necessarily supererogatory in this way, I do not mean to assert that there are kinds of action which are immune to criticism. When a monstrous sacrifice is made in order to obtain inconsequential benefits for someone else, we might properly condemn the sacrifice as foolish or, more strongly, idiotic; for it is not always appropriate to make a supererogatory gesture. My point is to contrast the supererogatory and the obligatory, not to create a class of actions for which an agent can invariably count on moral approval. The class of actions I have in mind are those that are supererogatory whenever they are appropriate. Nevertheless some advocates of natural rights, notably Locke, have held not only that it cannot be obligatory to give up the objects of inalienable rights but also that it is always wrong to do so (*The Second Treatise of Government*, sec. 23). Later in this chapter, reasons for thinking this prohibition unduly strong will be developed.

7. It is worth noting that self-defeating moral systems aimed at benign ends are conceivable. If a teleological system could be designed to achieve paradisal but completely uninhibited human relations in such a way that, once attained, this happy state would be permanent and the sober constraints of morality would never again be needed, this moral system would be self-defeating but, arguably, harmless. However, since moral systems of this kind can be dismissed as utopian speculation while twentieth century technology has made cataclysmic self-defeating moral systems all too real a possibility, my argument will focus on the latter type.

8. H. L. A. Hart and John Rawls also abjure self-defeating moral systems by appealing to their function. Hart categorically denies that moral systems can serve as the rules of suicide clubs, and Rawls urges that conflicting claims could not be satisfactorily adjudicated by a conception of justice prone to breaking down (*The Concept of Law*, p. 188, and A *Theory of Justice*, pp. 131–132).

9. For an account of how it is possible for many people reasonably to believe that killing can be obligatory, my negative criterion of adequacy notwithstanding, see chapter 3, section 7.

10. See chapter 4, sections 1–2 for an account of the obligation to tell the truth.

11. Rawls takes a similar view of supererogation. He characterizes supererogatory conduct as actions "that would be duties were not certain exempting conditions fulfilled which make allowance for reasonable self-interest" (A *Theory of Justice*, p. 439). Then he suggests that the bounds of reasonable self-interest must be determined from the standpoint of the original position. My argument against self-defeating moral systems and, in particular, against moral systems that can prescribe the destruction of moral agents can be read as fleshing out the reasoning about supererogation that would prevail in the original position. Certainly, maximin would recommend the exclusion of duties involving the destruction of moral agency. In situations in which some such destruction is inevitable, a person's being obligated to sacrifice himself or others' being obligated to sacrifice him is a worse predicament than that person's being permitted to sacrifice himself or others' being permitted to sacrifice him.

12. An argument to the effect that four rights which cannot be conscientiously renounced also cannot be renounced by fiat is made on independent grounds in chapter 5. However, it is worth noting at this point that the theory of inalienability presented so far supplies strong support for this result. Renunciation by fiat creates a universal simple permission with respect to the object of the renounced right; conscientious renunciation excepts only the renouncer from this simple permission. Notice, now, that any action which is itself morally neutral, i.e., simply permissible, is susceptible to moral transformation in either of two directions. Take the case of drinking water from an unowned spring. Just as the circumstance of a person's acquisition of the spring would render tapping it morally impermissible, the circumstance of needing to draw water from an unowned spring in order to save a life would render doing so morally compulsory. Any action which can be simply permissible could conceivably be obligatory. If some great goal would be advanced by doing it, if doing it were necessary to discharge a general duty, or if someone had promised to do it, the option to do it would yield to a requirement. Since both renunciation by fiat and conscientious renunciation generate simple permissions, renounceable rights either prohibit conduct the performance of which could be obligatory, or they enjoin conduct the nonperformance of which could be obligatory. If there are any obligations to inflict harm or to withhold aid which no

adequate moral system could prescribe, the rights protecting persons from these harms or assuring them of this level of aid are not renounceable. As we have seen, no moral system that is not self-defeating can impose an obligation to destroy moral agents. It follows that no right-holder can issue any simple permission that would authorize others to destroy his moral capacity and that the rights protecting persons from this form of injury are inalienable.

3. Four Inalienable Rights

1. Michael Walzer provides a helpful discussion of citizenship and self-sacrifice in *Obligations: Essays on Disobedience, War, and Citizenship*, pp. 77–98.

2. For a provocative discussion of coercion that parallels my treatment of the right to liberty in some respects but diverges in regard to the relation between law and coercion, see Virginia Held's "Coercion and Coercive Offers," pp. 49–62.

3. According to Rawls, justice requires recognition of an assortment of liberties including the right to vote, free speech, the right to hold property, and freedom from arbitrary arrest (A *Theory of Justice*, p. 61).

4. H. L. A. Hart criticizes the account of law as commands backed by threats (*The Concept of Law*, chs. 2–4). His discussion of obligation (chap. 5) is also relevant to the problem under consideration.

5. I have avoided explaining away legal interference in individuals' lives by appealing to the influence suffrage gives citizens over legislation in a democracy; for the will of the majority as it is embodied in the legislative process may conflict or coincide with the will of any given individual. Though it is desirable to have some input in this process, it is a mistake to conflate the impact of a vote with personal decision-making.

6. Respect for the rights to benign treatment and satisfaction of basic needs does not guarantee respect for the rights to life and personal liberty. Modern science confronts us with possibilities of painless killings and seizures of moral agency achieved without violating any right other than the right to life or the right to personal liberty. Nevertheless, it is important to recognize the secondary shield the rights to benign treatment and satisfaction of basic needs provide for the objects of the rights to life and personal liberty.

7. The right to medical treatment spans the right to benign treatment and the right to satisfaction of basic needs. Some medical treatment seems to be aimed mainly at alleviating the patient's agony or ridding her of the cause of it, whereas other types of treatment seem to be aimed mainly at preventing the patient's condition from deteriorating or improving it. Since the right to medical treatment can be divided between the right to benign treatment and the right to satisfaction of basic needs, it is best not to consolidate it into a single separate right because this would only serve to conflate different reasons for acknowledging the right.

8. For a more elaborate defense of the right to satisfaction of basic needs, see my "Human Rights in Pre-affluent Societies," pp. 139–144.

9. To avoid confusion, it is worth noting a situation in which a parent's interests can coincide with her child's although benign treatment is at issue. If a parent must undergo an extremely painful treatment in order to recover from a potentially fatal

illness, her own interest in self-preservation may move her to agree to the treatment, and coincidentally her recovery will eventually enable her to resume her parental duties. In this case, the parent's conduct cannot be considered supererogatory. However, if she genuinely would prefer to die rather than undergoing the treatment but chooses to submit to it purely out of a sense of responsibility for her child, her conduct would be supererogatory. Of course, the difficulty in separating altruistic from self-interested motives in a case like this would justify us in doubting anyone's claim that her submission to medical treatment was in fact an act of supererogation.

10. For a helpful general discussion of property rights, their limits, and their justifications, see Lawrence Becker's *Property Rights*.

11. See chapter 6, section 1 for a discussion of the moral position of the person whose right is abridged. Her obligation to respect others' rights to consume their allotments is at best quasi-moral.

12. See chapter 2, section 4 for an account of self-defeating moral systems and an explanation of their unacceptability.

4. Inalienable Rights and the Foundations of Moral Interaction

1. I disregard the possibility of exclusive liberties since they are not sufficiently distinguishable from rights in the case of the four rights under discussion. If a person is at liberty to be alive and to act unhampered by coercion or infliction of acute pain, and if others are barred from killing him, from forcing their wills upon him, or from torturing him, the right-holder enjoys the same protection as he would with rights to life, liberty, and benign treatment. Furthermore, if a person is at liberty to seek basic necessities and no one else is authorized to try to obtain the same goods, the right-holder in effect has a right to any supplies of the goods he requires that are accessible to him; the sole difference between his liberty and a right to these goods is that his liberty does not entitle him to demand that others provide them for him.

2. For the distinction between a right and a liberty and an account of alienating rights and liberties, see chapter 2, sections 1 and 2.

3. *Leviathan*, part I, chapter 13. In *Philosophical Explanations*, pp. 460–461, Robert Nozick seconds this point in urging that all moral systems must include a "nonavoidance condition" which prohibits persons from eluding moral obligations by destroying the property in virtue of which these obligations are owed.

4. *Leviathan*, chapter 15.

5. Some objections to Hobbes' account of inalienable rights are given in chapter 1, section 4.

6. The idea of renunciation by fiat is examined in chapter 2, section 1.

7. It is worth noting at this point that the claim that it is impossible for any adequate moral system to permit persons to renounce their rights to life, personal liberty, benign treatment, and satisfaction of basic needs is not equivalent to the claim that it is necessary for all moral systems to impose an absolute obligation to retain these rights. Circumstances so dire that possession of these rights would cease to have the slightest moral force are conceivable. In that case, persons would lose these rights

4. Foundations of Moral Interaction 203

willy-nilly, and any obligation to keep them would be canceled since it could not be fulfilled. Thus, there cannot be an absolute obligation to keep inalienable rights. But, more important, in these calamitous circumstances all moral systems would be inapplicable, for possession of these rights is necessary for moral agency and moral agency is necessary for moral compliance. As a result, these conduct codes could intelligibly be said neither to permit nor to prohibit the voiding of inalienable rights; their directives have been silenced by circumstances.

    8. The ways in which these forms of affliction compromise moral agency are detailed in chapter 3, sections 1 and 3.

    9. I consider the question of whether a system of duties could duplicate the set of inalienable rights in chapter 6, sections 8 and 9.

    10. If I had contended that the right to property should count as an inalienable right, fines would be direct infringements of this right. But since I have substituted the right to satisfaction of basic needs for the right to property, fines need not actually infringe this right though they may force the person to rely on others for satisfaction of her basic needs. Still, it is possible for a fine to infringe a person's right to satisfaction of basic needs. If a person cannot find employment as a result of a sensational trial, has no friends or family to take care of her, cannot find a benefactor, and lives in a state that only recognizes the right to acquire property as a means of securing the right to satisfaction of basic needs, a fine that consumes her savings and investments would infringe her right to satisfaction of basic needs. If we suppose that she is the first resident who has proved unable to satisfy her basic needs by exercising her right to property, we cannot condemn the state for failing to have established a welfare system.

    11. For detailed consideration of the link between enforcement and respect for victims' rights, see chapter 6, section 3.

    12. Kant, *Foundations*, pp. 403 and 422. Marcus Singer also makes this point (*Generalization in Ethics*, p. 231). Even Locke accords honesty special importance; like the duties that confer natural rights, "truth and the keeping of faith belongs to men, as men, and not as members of society" (*The Second Treatise of Government*, section 14).

    13. Melden, "Action," p. 68.

    14. In *1984*, George Orwell depicts a society governed by a regime that systematically flouts the prohibition on deception. The protagonist, Winston Smith, knows that the government of Oceania routinely forges historical documents to suit its purposes, but he yearns for a tangible proof that this is so. Thus, he cherishes a scrap of old newspaper reporting an event subsequently denied by the regime because he sees in it a clue to exposing the rest of the regime's lies. It is worth noting, however, that evidence decisively confirming the regime's veracity in some regard, for example, that Oceania really was allied with Eurasia and fighting a war with Eastasia, could also have served as a basis for decoding the political system.

    15. Needless to say, it is possible that our apparently reliable world is contained within an all-inclusive system of deceit constructed so that we can never discover the nature of our delusion. Descartes' Evil Genius may be in control though we do not suspect it. Still, within the world to which we do have access deceit occurs against a background of honesty and regularity. Consequently, we are able to decipher our own actions as well as the actions of others.

    16. John Rawls seems to have something like this distinction in mind when he proposes a tripartite division of principles of justice. First, there are principles that would be rejected in the original position, e.g., first person egoism and utilitarianism;

these correspond to the category of invidious rescission by design because adherence to them impedes progress toward true justice. Then, there are principles that would be chosen in the original position, namely, Rawls' package of equal liberties, fair equality of opportunity, and the difference principle; these constitute a wholly satisfactory theory of justice. And finally there is a principle that promotes conditions favorable to eventual implementation of Rawls' two principles of justice, namely, his general conception of justice which allows trade-offs forbidden by the special conception of justice; this is the analogue of the category of benign rescission by design. Though circumstances may warrant adherence to a moral system belonging to this third category, Rawls explicitly regards such measures as temporary (A *Theory of Justice*, pp. 151–152 and 247).

5. Possession of Inalienable Rights

1. For the sake of simplicity, I leave aside the theological complications of Locke's view and stress his affirmation of the similarity of human faculties and his concern with the possibility of premature death (*The Second Treatise of Government*, sections 4 and 6).

2. H. J. McCloskey construes the capacity to benefit in terms of interests ("Rights," pp. 125–126). Also, Robert Nozick's discussion of the treatment of animals implicitly appeals to the ability of animals to benefit from what he calls stringent side constraints which are constitutive of rights (*Anarchy, State, and Utopia*, pp. 35–42). For an illuminating general discussion of the relation between rights and benefits, see David Lyons, "Rights, Claimants, and Beneficiaries," pp. 173–185.

3. The arguments that follow parallel and supplement Rawls' discussion of the capacity for moral personality as a range property (A *Theory of Justice*, pp. 504–512).

4. It could be objected that a system of differential inalienable rights is precisely what any penal institution establishes since judicial sentences authorize abridgment of convicted criminals' rights. Nevertheless, two features of penal institutions distinguish them from the system of graduated inalienable rights contemplated here. First, trials consider allegations regarding particular acts; they do not attempt to decide whether agents are good or bad. Second, punishments corresponding in severity to the crime committed specify definite ways in which the convict's rights can be abridged; they do not simply nullify or downgrade the stringency of his rights. As I shall argue in chapter 6, sections 3–6, penal sanctions, when properly administered, respect the inalienable rights of perpetrators and their victims alike.

5. It is worth noting that, according to Locke, we have duties to our divine creator which invariably supersede our natural rights and which bind each of us "to preserve himself and not to quit his station wilfully" (*The Second Treatise of Government*, sec. 6). But, as I have urged, it is possible for a person to sacrifice the objects of inalienable rights supererogatorily (chapter 2, sections 6 and 7).

6. *Anarchy, State, and Utopia*, pp. 42–45.

7. Ibid., p. 44.

8. I leave aside the suggestion that the result machines themselves are potential moral agents which are activated by the transferral of the tank dwellers' agency and which then merit moral consideration in their own right. Since creation of a set of

6. Permissible Abridgment

mechanical moral agents reveals nothing about the propriety of extinguishing moral potential, I shall assume that result machines merely simulate moral agency.

9. I leave aside two important questions: 1) whether animals have alienable rights, and 2) what arguments independent of rights might be given for protecting wildlife.

6. Permissible Abridgment

1. I will use the term 'denial' to refer to a wrongful refusal to recognize a person's rights, the term 'violation' to refer to a wrongful refusal to respect a person's rights, and the term 'infringement' to refer to a permissible refusal to honor a person's right-based claims. I use the term 'abridgment' generically. Here I follow Judith Jarvis Thomson, "Self-Defense and Rights."

2. I reserve the question of enforcement, that is, the question of what right-holders may do to cope with violations of their rights, for sections 3–6 of this chapter.

3. See chapter 3, section 4 for the full account of this society.

4. Needless to say, slave owners have sometimes placated their chattels by granting "well-behaved" ones special privileges, and they have also sometimes succeeded in instilling in their slaves affection and loyalty toward themselves. These favored slaves may become ambivalent about their position: they may be neither abjectly nor tactically submissive, but rather torn between self-respect and regard for their masters. However, because attractive egoistic incentives have never been and could not be the mainstay of social control in slave societies, slaves who have been taken into their masters' confidence can be regarded as an exceptional phenomenon.

5. Mill distinguishes the obligations correlative to rights from other moral requirements by arguing that the former are enforceable (*Utilitarianism*, chap. 5). Along similar lines, H. L. A. Hart contends that the central conceptual habitat of rights language is the law with its background of coercive institutions ("Are There Any Natural Rights?" pp. 175–176). In keeping with this tradition, Robert Nozick assumes that natural rights authorize punishing transgressors and argues at length that a minimal state can justifiably perform this function (*Anarchy, State, and Utopia*, chaps. 1–6).

6. The compatibility of sanctions and the right to personal liberty is discussed in chapter 3, section 2.

7. For a related treatment of punishment, see Joel Feinberg, "The Expressive Function of Punishment," pp. 25–34.

8. For the distinction between transferal of a right and paternal exercise of a right, see chapter 1, section 3.

9. See Robert Nozick's suggestive remarks on the problem of punishing the guilty for bad reasons (*Anarchy, State, and Utopia*, pp. 105–108).

10. In this connection, it is important to note that a liability to punishment is not equivalent to a duty to submit to punishment. To say that a person is morally liable to punishment is to say only that she is not morally exempt from it (W. N. Hohfeld, *Fundamental Legal Conceptions*, pp. 59–61).

11. Once the apparatus of state-run trials is in place, an additional complication arises with respect to legal counsel. Needless to say, if defendants are assigned

incompetent lawyers or deprived of legal advice, their rights are violated. But assuming that defendants have access to adequate attorneys, nothing more can be done to protect them from their lawyers' intellectual oversights or rhetorical miscalculations.

12. If we imagine a small, cohesive society, it is possible to defend an enforcement system in which procedures are not codified and no institution claims to monopolize or delegate legitimate force. However, it is important to recognize that less formal enforcement systems are only acceptable when social conditions supplement these arrangements so as to provide a guaranteed equivalent to institutional ones. For example, a community's social relations could be so transparent to its members and social pressure could be so effective a force within the group that judicial impeachment procedures would not be necessary: judges could be relied upon to disqualify themselves. The scale of modern societies prevents them from meeting the conditions that would allow them to dispense with the state. For further consideration of the contrast between tribal societies and modern ones, see section 7 of this chapter.

13. It might be suggested that convicts could be required to compensate their victims and thus to respect their rights. Setting aside questions about the intelligibility of compensation for being murdered, enduring torture, and the like, as a practical matter inalienable rights violations are plainly so serious that their perpetrators rarely have the means to make restitution to their victims. If compensation were the only way that victims' rights could be respected, their rights would usually be abridged by default. But the obligation to respect inalienable rights cannot be dissolved by the vagaries of convicts' financial fortunes, and unless the state is complicit in the criminals' actions, there is no reason for the state to defray these costs. Consequently, institutions for punishing criminals must be maintained, and compensation must be relegated to a supplemental role.

14. In *Crime and Punishment*, Dostoevsky portrays Raskolnikov as an individual driven to expiate his crime through confession and submission to punishment.

15. The latter possibility corresponds roughly to what Aristotle dubs "equity" as distinguished from "justice" (*Nicomachean Ethics*, 1137b).

16. See chapter 3, section 3 for a response to the objection that rights to benign treatment and satisfaction of basic needs make intolerable demands on available resources.

17. For a sketch of the relation between inalienable rights and property rights, see chapter 3, section 5.

18. The burgeoning literature on international responsibility and rights is much too extensive to cite in detail. Henry Shue's *Basic Rights* provides a helpful examination of this topic.

19. See section 4 of this chapter for an account of structural violations of inalienable rights through private enforcement.

20. Both Joel Feinberg and Richard Wasserstrom use this approach. See Feinberg's "The Nature and Value of Rights" and Wasserstrom's "Rights, Human Rights, and Racial Discrimination," p. 123. Ronald Dworkin shares Feinberg's and Wasserstrom's perception of theories based on duties as agent-centered and theories based on rights as attending primarily to the potential victim (*Taking Rights Seriously*, p. 172).

21. For a complementary discussion of the related problem of whether utilitarianism can accommodate legal rights, see David Lyons' "Utility and Rights," p. 107.

22. Many philosophers have pointed out that religious accounts of obligations separate the person toward whom the obligatory conduct is directed from the

transcendent entity to whom the obligation is owed. Joel Feinberg makes this point in his comments on the paper by Richard Wasserstrom cited above, and he uses this idea in his description of Nowheresville ("Wasserstrom on Human Rights" and "The Nature and Value of Rights," pp. 247–249). H. L. A. Hart, too, distinguishes between obligations owed to a divine being and ones owed to persons ("Are There Any Natural Rights?" p. 182). What I have said in regard to theological ethics would also apply to a theory of obligation based on political authority or on an idea of self-perfection.

7. Contract Theory and Inalienable Rights

1. Rawls, "Kantian Constructivism," p. 519.
2. Rawls' remarks on this question are scattered throughout A *Theory of Justice*. See, for example, pp. 151–152, 248, 276, and 542–543.
3. I leave aside the much discussed questions about contract theory's role in rationalizing the rise of a capitalist bourgeoisie.
4. Justified emigration, it should be noted, does not presuppose inalienable rights violations. Persons ought to be free to relocate for reasons no more momentous than a preference for another climate or landscape. Nevertheless, if circumstances somehow overrule comparatively frivolous grounds for emigration, the force of inalienable rights violations as a justification for emigration would not be diminished. In a similar vein, it should be emphasized that inalienable rights violations are not the only form of injustice that can provide a compelling justification for rebellion. Evidently, the neatness of the link between the right of self-defense as a form of rights assertion, on the one hand, and emigration and revolution as responses to inalienable rights violations, on the other, has highlighted the role of fundamental rights in justifying activities aimed at gaining liberation.

Bibliography

Bandman, Bertram. "Rights and Claims." *Journal of Value Inquiry* (1973), 7:204–213.
Baumrin, Bernard H. "Prima Facie Duties." *Journal of Philosophy* (1965), 62:736–739.
Becker, Lawrence. *Property Rights*. Boston: Routledge and Kegan Paul, 1977.
Bedau, Hugo. "The Right to Life." *The Monist* (1968), 52:550–572.
Blackstone, W. T. "Equality and Human Rights." *The Monist* (1968), 52:616–639.
Brandt, Richard B. *Ethical Theory*. Englewood Cliffs, N.J.: Prentice-Hall, 1959.
Brown, Stuart M., Jr. "Inalienable Rights." *Philosophical Review* (1955), 64:192–211.
Carritt. E. F. *Ethical and Political Thinking*. London: Oxford University Press, 1947.
―――― *Morals and Politics*. London: Oxford University Press, 1935.
Cranston, Maurice. "Human Rights, Real and Supposed." In D. D. Raphael, ed., *Political Theory and the Rights of Man*, pp. 43–53. Bloomington: Indiana University Press, 1967.
―――― *What Are Human Rights?* New York: Taplinger, 1973.
Dworkin, Ronald. *Taking Rights Seriously*. Cambridge: Harvard University Press, 1977.
Feinberg, Joel. "Duties, Rights, and Claims." *American Philosophical Quarterly* (1966), 3:137–144.
―――― "The Expressive Function of Punishment." In Gertrude Ezorsky, ed., *Philosophical Perspectives on Punishment*, pp. 25–34. Albany: State University of New York Press, 1972.
―――― "The Nature and Value of Rights." *Journal of Value Inquiry* (1970), 4:243–260.
―――― *Social Philosophy*. Englewood Cliffs, N.J.: Prentice-Hall, 1973.
―――― "Voluntary Euthanasia and the Inalienable Right to Life." *Philosophy and Public Affairs* (1978), 7:93–123.
―――― "Wasserstrom on Human Rights" *Journal of Philosophy* (1964), 61:641–645.

Fishkin, James S. *Tyranny and Legitimacy*. Baltimore: Johns Hopkins University Press, 1979.
Frankena, W. K. "The Concept of Universal Human Rights." In *Science, Language, and Human Rights*, pp. 189–207. Philadelphia: University of Pennsylvania Press, 1952.
———. *Ethics*, 2d ed. Englewood Cliffs, N.J.: Prentice-Hall, 1973.
———. "Natural and Inalienable Rights." *Philosophical Review* (1955), 64:212–232.
Gert, Bernard. "Hobbes and Psychological Egoism." In Bernard H. Baumrin, ed., *Hobbes's "Leviathan,"* pp. 107–126. Belmont, Calif.: Wadsworth, 1969.
Gewirth, Alan. "Categorial Consistency in Ethics." *Philosophical Quarterly* (1967), 17:289–299.
———. *Reason and Morality*. Chicago: University of Chicago Press, 1978.
Golding, Martin P. "Ethical Issues in Biological Engineering." *UCLA Law Review* (1968), 15:443–479.
———. "Towards a Theory of Human Rights." *The Monist* (1968), 52:521–549.
Green, T.H. *Lectures on the Principles of Political Obligation*. Ann Arbor: University of Michigan Press, 1967.
Hare, R.M. *Freedom and Reason*. London: Oxford University Press, 1963.
Hart, H. L. A. "Are There Any Natural Rights?" *Philosophical Review* (1955), 64:175–191.
———. "The Ascription of Responsibility and Rights." In Anthony Flew, ed., *Essays on Logic and Language*, pp. 145–166. Oxford: Basil Blackwell, 1951.
———. *The Concept of Law*. London: Oxford University Press, 1961.
Held, Virginia. "Coercion and Coercive Offers." In J. Roland Pennock and John W. Chapman, eds., *Nomos* 14, pp. 49–62. Chicago: Aldine and Atherton, 1972.
Hobbes, Thomas. *Leviathan*. Baltimore: Penguin, 1972.
Hohfeld, Wesley Newcomb. *Fundamental Legal Conceptions*. New Haven: Yale University Press, 1919.
Kant, Immanuel. *Foundations of the Metaphysics of Morals*. Translated by Lewis White Beck. New York: The Bobbs-Merrill Company, Inc., 1959.
Locke, John. *The Second Treatise of Government*. Indianapolis: Hackett, 1980.
———. "Selections from An Essay Concerning Human Understanding." In *British Moralists*, pp. 326–347. Edited by L.A. Selby-Bigge. New York: The Bobbs-Merril Company, Inc., 1964.
Lyons, David. "The Correlativity of Rights and Duties." *Nous* (1970), 4:45–55.
———. "Human Rights and the General Welfare." In David Lyons, ed.,*Rights*, pp. 174–186. Belmont, Calif.: Wadsworth, 1979.
———. "Rights, Claimants, and Beneficiaries." *American Philosophical Quarterly* (1969), 6:173–185.
———. "Utility and Rights." NOMOS (1982), 24:107–138.
———. "Utility as a Possible Ground of Rights." *Nous* (1980), 14:17–28.
McCloskey, H.J. "Human Needs, Rights and Political Values." *American Philosophical Quarterly* (1976), 13:1–11.

Bibliography

―――― "Rights." *Philosophical Quarterly* (1965), 15:115–127.
―――― "The Right to Life." *Mind* (1975), 84:403–425.
MacDonald, Margaret. "Natural Rights." In A.I. Melden, ed., *Human Rights*, pp. 40–60. Belmont, Calif.: Wadsworth, 1970.
Melden, A. I. "Action." In Donald F. Gustafson, ed., *Essays in Philosophical Psychology*, pp. 58–76. New York: Doubleday, 1964.
―――― "The Concept of Universal Human Rights." In *Science, Language and Human Rights*, pp. 167–187. Philadelphia: University of Pennsylvania Press, 1952.
―――― "The Play of Rights." *The Monist* (1972), 56:479–502.
―――― *Rights and Right Conduct*. New York: Humanities Press, 1970.
Meyers, Diana T. "Human Rights in Pre-affluent Societies." *Philosophical Quarterly* (1981), 31:139–144.
―――― "The Inevitability of the State." *Analysis* (1981), 41:46–49.
―――― "The Rationale for Inalienable Rights in Moral Systems." *Social Theory and Practice* (1981), 7:127–144.
Morris, Herbert. "Persons and Punishment." In A. I. Melden, ed., *Human Rights*, pp. 111–134. Belmont, Calif.: Wadsworth, 1970.
Narveson, Jan. "Commentary on 'The Nature and Value of Rights.'" *Journal of Value Inquiry* (1970), 4:258–260.
Nielson, Kai. "Scepticism and Human Rights." *The Monist* (1968), 52:573–594.
Nozick, Robert. *Anarchy, State, and Utopia*. New York: Basic Books, 1974.
―――― *Philosophical Explanations*. Cambridge: Harvard University Press, 1981.
Plamenatz, J.P. *Consent, Freedom and Political Obligation*, 2d ed. London: Oxford University Press, 1968.
Raphael, D.D. "Human Rights, Old and New." In D. D. Raphael, ed., *Political Theory and the Rights of Man*, pp. 54–67. Bloomington: Indiana University Press, 1967.
―――― "The Rights of Man and the Rights of the Citizen." In D. D. Raphael, ed., *Political Theory and the Rights of Man*, pp. 101–118. Bloomington: Indiana University Press, 1967.
Rawls, John. "Kantian Constructivism in Moral Theory: The Dewey Lectures 1980." *Journal of Philosophy* (1980), 77:515–572.
―――― *A Theory of Justice*. Cambridge: Harvard University Press, 1971.
Richards, B.A. "Inalienable Rights: Recent Criticism and Old Doctrine." *Philosophy and Phenomenological Research* (1968–1969), 29:391–404.
Ritchie, D.G. *Natural Rights*. New York: Macmillan, 1895.
Ross, W.D. *The Right and the Good*. London: Oxford University Press, 1930.
Rousseau, Jean Jacques. *Emile*. Barbara Foxley, tr. New York: Dutton, 1974.
―――― *The Social Contract*. New York: Hafner, 1947.
Schwartz, Adina. "Against Universality." *Journal of Philosophy* (1981), 78:127–143.
Shue, Henry. *Basic Rights*. Princeton: Princeton University Press, 1980.
Singer, Marcus. *Generalization in Ethics*. New York: Knopf, 1961.
Taurek, John M. "Should the Numbers Count?" *Philosophy and Public Affairs* (1977), 6:293–316.

Thomson, Judith Jarvis. "Rights and Compensation." *Nous* (1980), 14:3–15.
―――. "Self-Defense and Rights." *The Lindley Lecture*. University of Kansas, 1976.
―――. "Some Ruminations on Rights." *Arizona Law Review* (1977), 19:45–60.
Vlastos, Gregory. "Justice and Equality." In A. I. Melden, ed., *Human Rights*, pp. 76–95. Belmont, Calif.: Wadsworth, 1970.
Walzer, Michael. *Obligations: Essays on Disobedience, War, and Citizenship*. New York: Simon and Schuster, 1970.
Wasserstrom, Richard. "Rights, Human Rights, and Racial Discrimination." In James Rachels, ed., *Moral Problems*, pp. 109–124. New York: Harper and Row, 1971.

Index

Absolute rights and obligations, 2–3, 4, 10–11, 20, 31, 46, 143, 169, 197*n*1, 198*n*8, 202*n*7
Altruism, 35–37, 51–52, 74–76, 78–81, 97, 178, 201*n*9
Amorality, 41, 102–11, 189
Animals, 117–21, 128, 136–40, 205*n*9
Autonomy, 8–9, 74–75, 111, 185, 186, 201*n*5; *see also* Moral agency

Basic needs, *see* Satisfaction of basic needs
Benign treatment, right to, 169–75, 201*n*6, 201*n*7; content, 53, 63; and moral agency, 63, 114; and supererogation, 65–66, 71–76

Catastrophe, 40–43, 46, 86–87, 125–27, 134, 145, 179, 202*n*7
Children, 46, 120, 128–36, 139
Consent, 31–32, 71–76, 156, 189, 197*n*6
Consistency, 17, 50–51, 198*n*13
Criteria of adequacy, for moral systems, 17–18, 145, 176, 184–85, 198*n*13; *see also* Rescission by design; Self-defeatism

Deceit, 49–50, 87, 99; impenetrable, 100–11, 203*n*14, 203*n*15; justification for, 93–98, 112

Deontological ethics, 37, 176–79, 181
Deprivation, 63–64, 67–68, 84, 99, 135, 158, 164, 178; *see also* Satisfaction of basic needs, right to

Ecological roles, 136–40
Egoism, 86, 92–93, 102, 105–6, 147–49, 150, 151–52, 176, 190, 205*n*4
Equality, 122–27, 176, 179, 180–81
Experience machine, the, 131–36, 139, 204*n*8

Gewirth, Alan, 198*n*13
Goals, social, 7, 16–17, 178; supramoral, 38, 39
Goodness, of morality, 37, 38, 40, 42, 44; of persons, 124–27, 177–78
Green, T. H., 198*n*12

Hart, H. L. A., 200*n*8, 201*n*4
Hobbes, Thomas, 85–86, 186, 188–90, 192, 194, 198*n*10
Honesty, *see* Obligation to engage in non-deceitful relations
Human rights, 1, 115, 129

Ideals, personal, 77–78, 147–49
Impartiality, 121, 148, 158–59, 163
Inalienable rights, 1–2, 7–9, 15, 35, 45,

214　Index

Inalienable rights (*Continued*)
　51–52, 89–91, 111–14, 115–16, 141, 184–85, 188, 197n1; contrasted with absolute rights, 2–4, 20, 143, 197n1, 202n7; criteria for, 52, 85, 87, 114; qualifications for possession of, 116–22, 124–25, 133, 150–52; and renunciation, 9–15, 34, 51–52, 83–84, 87, 114, 200n12; traditional accounts of, 16–21, 86, 183–87
Individualism, 196; economic, 192–94; moral, 44, 184–85, 186–87; political, 194–96
Innocent convict, the problem of, 159–62
International morality, 173–75
Intuition, 19, 48, 52

Justice, 49–51, 58–60, 61, 165, 191–92; *see also* Rights, procedural respect

Kant, Immanuel, 100, 102, 176, 186–87
Killing, 46, 47–48, 50, 84, 94, 99, 118, 135, 147–48, 178; *see also* Life, right to

Liberties, 24; Hohfeldian, 26–34, 199n3; inalienable, 83–93, 95, 98–99, 103, 111–14; Rawlsian, 58, 201n3
Liberty, *see* Personal liberty, right to
Life, right to, 57–62, 64–65, 118–20, 146, 201n6; content, 53, 54; and moral agency, 54, 114; and supererogation, 54–55, 72–73
Locke, John, 118, 153, 183–86, 188–91, 193, 194, 198n11, 199n6, 203n12, 204n1, 204n5

Medical care, right to, 169, 172, 201n7
Metaprescription, enjoining compliance with moral directives, 37–44
Moral agency, 20, 38, 52, 88, 102, 115, 122–23; and deceit, 102–11, 134; destruction of, 41–51, 75, 86, 111, 131, 144, 155, 200n11; and inalienable rights, 51–52, 76, 87, 98–99, 121–27, 151–52, 177; *see also* Benign treatment, right to; Life, right to; Personal liberty, right to; Satisfaction of basic needs, right to
Moral education, right to, 129–31, 135–36, 137
Moral incompetency, 13, 120, 128, 134, 141

Moral interaction, 20, 37, 39–46, 86–87, 89, 100–1, 103–7, 114, 121, 131, 134, 140, 146, 150–52, 182, 196
Moral potential, 42, 129, 134–36, 141, 151
Moral responsibility, 38–39, 41, 42, 44, 47, 76, 102–3, 107–11, 124–25, 134, 149, 184, 187, 196
Moral systems, 17–21, 37–44, 77, 80–81, 86–87, 96–97, 113–14, 175–82, 186

Natural rights, 1, 183–86, 191, 192–94
Nozick, Robert, 131, 198n15, 202n3

Obligation to engage in nondeceitful relations, 49, 87, 93, 98, 99, 109–10, 111–13
Obligations, as substitutes for rights, 120, 176–82; *see also* Permissibility, and obligation; Rights, respect
Orwell, George, 203n14

Permissibility, 77, 80, 83–84, 88–91, 144; and obligation, 48–51, 74–75, 168–69, 177–78, 200n12; types of, 24–25, 31–32, 98
Person, concept of, 16–17, 198n15; *see also* Moral agency
Personal codes, 77–81
Personal liberty, right to, 62, 64–65, 70, 146, 150–52, 201n6; and coercion, 56–62; content, 53, 55; and moral agency, 55, 58–60, 114; and supererogation, 55–56, 73–76
Prima facie rights, 5; *see also* Absolute rights and obligations; Inalienable rights, contrasted with absolute rights; Permissibility
Promises, 71–76
Property, 30–31, 66, 68–71, 93, 172, 179, 193–94, 203n10
Psychology, 16–17, 89–90, 141, 149, 159
Punishment, 90–91, 96, 144, 154, 156, 166–69, 204n4, 205n10

Rawls, John, 187–88, 191–92, 198n15, 200n8, 200n11, 203n16, 204n3
Rebellion, 194–95
Renunciation, 9–15, 23–34, 135, 198n9; by fiat, 26–28, 32–34, 52, 83–84, 87, 114,

Index

200n12; conscientious, 26, 28–35, 51–52, 83–84, 114, 200n12; partial, 34, 84
Rescission by design, 138–40, 145, 151; defined, 86; and inalienable rights, 87, 111, 113–14, 121, 125, 134, 185; why inadmissible, 87, 150, 184
Rights, 36, 120, 127; abridgment, 6, 31–32, 35, 61, 64–65, 113, 124, 144–49, 205n1; assertion, 5, 7–8, 32, 120, 153–56, 163, 175, 176, 190, 197n6; and compensation, 147, 149, 154–55, 206n13; denial, 28, 96, 98, 144, 149–52, 205n1; enforcement, 152–75, 179–80, 194–95, 206n12 (*see also* Punishment; Rights, assertion; State, the); forfeiture, 9, 13–15, 69, 126, 166; infringement, 5, 32, 96, 144–49, 152, 158, 164, 166, 177–79, 197n4, 205n1; possession, 4–9, 33, 115–22; procedural respect, 5–7, 146–47, 148, 157, 159–61, 163–65, 205n11; renunciation, *see* Renunciation; respect, 3–4, 7, 96, 120–21, 133, 144–49, 155, 158, 164–65, 168–69, 170–75; revocation, 9, 13–15, 126, 135; structural violation, 161–62, 165, 174; transfer, 9, 11–13, 25, 155–56; violation, 32, 56–58, 87, 91, 98, 120, 144, 147, 148, 152, 154, 156, 157–60, 164, 165–67, 194–95, 205n1; waiver, 9, 11–13, 25
Rousseau, Jean-Jacques, 184–86, 188–91, 192, 194

Satisfaction of basic needs, right to, 146, 169–75, 179, 193–94, 201n6, 201n7, 203n10; content, 53, 63, 68–71; and moral agency, 64, 114; and scarcity, 64–65; and supererogation, 66–68, 71–76
Schwartz, Adina, 198n15
Security, 11, 52, 84, 88–93, 98, 112–13, 156, 177, 196

Self-defeatism, 37–51, 80, 138, 140, 145, 200n11; contrasted with rescission by design, 86–87; defined, 37–45; and inalienable liberties, 84–85, 155–56, 185; and inalienable rights, 44–45, 51–52, 121, 125, 130; why inadmissible, 38–44, 46–48, 150, 184, 200n7
Self-defense, 85, 88, 92–93, 95–98, 144, 152, 153–55, 158–59, 162–63, 194–95
Self-perpetuation, of moral systems, 45–46, 130, 145
Self-respect, 78–79, 176
Self-sacrifice, 37, 45, 49, 51, 66–67, 71–76, 126–27, 178–79, 200n11; and risk, 54, 71, 85, 111–13
State, the, 60–62, 153, 155–57, 160–61, 163–65, 168–69, 172–73, 174–75, 179, 189–91
State of nature, 188–90, 192–93, 196
Subjugation, 55–56, 73–74, 84, 88, 93–95, 99, 135, 150–52, 158, 178, 205n4; *see also* Personal liberty, right to
Supererogation, 34–37, 45, 51–52, 71–76, 85, 96, 97, 113, 178, 199n6, 200n11; *see also* Benign treatment, right to; Life, right to; Personal liberty, right to; Satisfaction of basic needs, right to

Teleological ethics, 37–38, 46, 105–6, 176, 178, 181
Torture, 46, 55–56, 65–66, 84, 95, 99, 135, 150, 178; *see also* Benign treatment, right to

Universality, 2, 4, 77–80, 116, 141, 176, 188

Values, 77–78, ultimate, 45–47
Victims, acknowledgment of, 6, 153–55, 165–67

GPSR Authorized Representative: Easy Access System Europe, Mustamäe tee 50, 10621 Tallinn, Estonia, gpsr.requests@easproject.com